C000053282

GREAT FOOTBALL HEADLINES

GREAT FOOTBALL HEADLINES

A Scrapbook of Headlines from the Back Pages

First published in Great Britain in 2002 by
Michael O'Mara Books Limited
9 Lion Yard, Tremadoc Road
London SW4 7NQ

Copyright © Michael O'Mara Books Ltd, 2002

All rights reserved. No part of this publication may be reproduced, stored in a retrieval system, or transmitted by any means, without the prior permission in writing of the publisher, nor be otherwise circulated in any form of binding or cover other than that in which it is published and without a similar condition including this condition being imposed on the subsequent purchaser.

A CIP catalogue record for this book is available from the British Library

ISBN 1-85479-897-9

1 3 5 7 9 10 8 6 4 2

Designed and typeset by Design 23

www.mombooks.com

Printed and bound in Slovenia by Printing House Delo Tiskarna by arrangement with Presernova Druzba D.D.

Extracts, headlines and pictures from the *Daily Mail, The Times, Sunday Times, Sun, News of the World, Guardian, Observer, Sunday Mirror, Mirror, People, Daily Express* and *Sunday Express* are reproduced with the kind permission of, respectively, Atlantic Syndication, News International Syndication, Guardian & Observer Syndication, Mirror Group Newspapers and Express Syndication.

Individual credits: *Guardian* © pp.22-3 – report by Victor Zorza; pp.71, 81 – reports by Albert Barham; p.89 – report by Paul Wilcox; p.92 – report by David Lacey

CONTENTS

WEMBLEY STADIUM HOSTS FIRST CUP FINAL

WEMBLEY STADIUM STORMED BY EXCITED CUP FINAL CROWDS

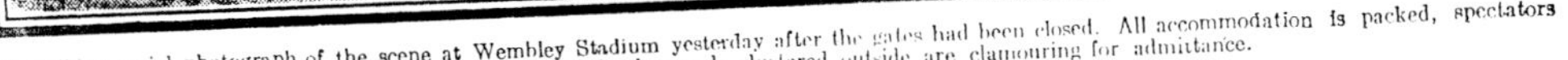

A striking aerial photograph of the scene at Wembley Stadium yesterday after the gates had been closed. All accommodation is packed, spectators flood the playing pitch, while thousands clustered outside are clamouring for admittance.

One of four daring souls who climbed a drain-pipe to secure an entrance at the back of the lofty covered stand.

Police holding back would-be spectators at the entrance to the tunnel leading to the pitch.

Police arriving by motor-van at the ground in response to a call for reinforcements.

The crowd swarming over the closed turnstiles heedless of the instruction to "Pay Here."

The most amazing Cup final on record was won by Bolton Wanderers yesterday, when they defeated West Ham United by two clear goals at the Empire Stadium, Wembley. The start was delayed for three-quarters of an hour by the most extraordinary scenes. The gates were closed with thousands still waiting for admission, though the spectators within had broken through to the running track around the ground and invaded the playing pitch itself. The crowd outside rushed the ground, clambering over the turnstiles, and made the confusion even greater. With the arrival of the King, mounted police managed to get the pitch just clear. Pictures of play on page 24.

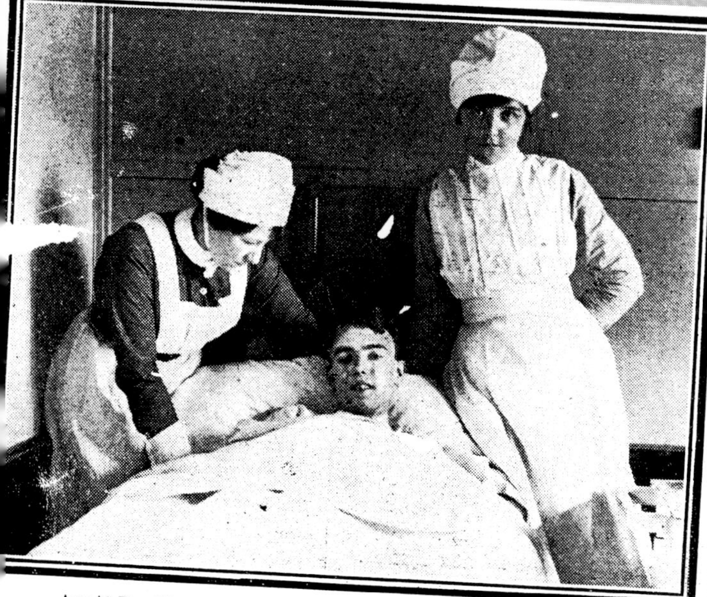

Arnold Ratcliffe, of Bolton. He was crushed and picked up unconscious.

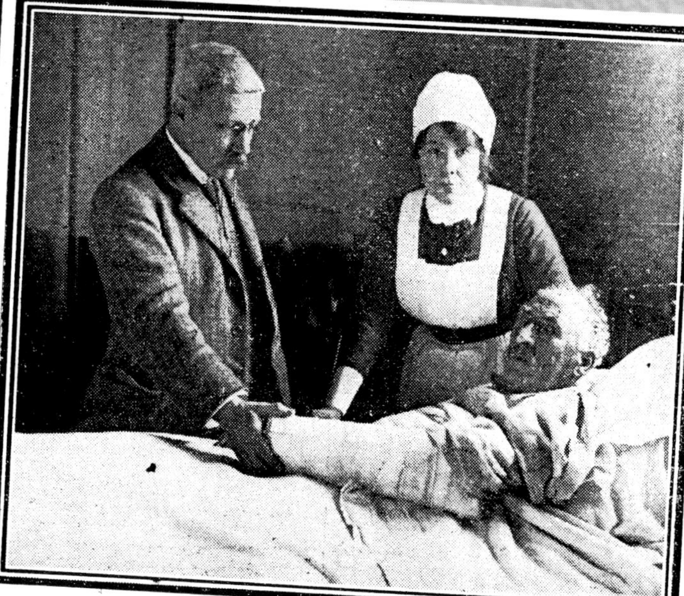

Thomas McGrigor, of Islington, in hospital with a broken arm and leg.

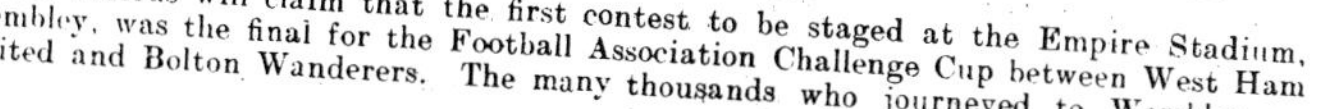

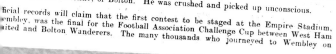

ficial records will claim that the first contest to be staged at the Empire Stadium, embley, was the final for the Football Association Challenge Cup between West Ham ited and Bolton Wanderers. The many thousands who journeyed to Wembley on Saturday will, however, long retain the memory of an earlier struggle in which the opposing elements were police and public, the ultimate victory resting with the force, whose untiring efforts eventually produced order from utter chaos.

VEMBLEY PARK SCENES.

SIR FRANK SWETTENHAM'S EXPERIENCES.

TO THE EDITOR OF THE TIMES.

Sir,—About two months ago, in esponse to an invitation from the Exhibion management, I applied for tickets to itness the final game in the Football up Tie. I received the tickets—which ere for numbered seats in a numbered ow of Block FF—and made my way ver a very rough cindered road from the ew Exhibition Station of the G.C. Railay to the Stadium.

Enormous crowds of people were then -2.45 p.m.—in the grounds and in the uter passages of the Stadium, and I oticed boards with rather confusing irections as to how to find the hidden locks of seats within. Directions to standing room" were seen everywhere, nd later experience showed rather unsual facilities for the occupation of eserved seats by those who had not paid r them, whilst the ticket-holders were ut out or left to find the seats as best ey could. I discovered a turnstile hich was said to lead to Block FF, and ere I gave up one portion of my ticket. aving passed the turnstile, a steep aircase led to a landing and a small oor giving access to the upper tiers of e Stadium. The staircase was crowded nd the landing blocked by a mass of eople, whose further progress was opped by a civilian and a constable at e doorway. After some time, the mmed mass determined to get in, and ushed through the doorway, thrusting e keepers aside. I was carried in as y a tidal wave—considerable squeezing, ut no real damage.

Once inside, and looking down from a great height, the scene was curious. The football ground was occupied by thousands of people, standing or walking about. No grass was visible, and only the tops of the goal-posts; but on the running track, at both ends of the ellipse, there were large empty spaces, showing that great masses of people had left positions from which they could see nothing and had walked on to the playing ground. In the tiers upon tiers of uncovered seats rising from the ground to the skyline, there could only be seen faces and headgear, a sloping mass of colour-wash in red and yellow, red faces and yellow caps. Having studied this strange picture with much interest, I began to search for my block and my seat. There were indications of other blocks—EE and GG—but FF escaped me; perhaps it had gone down in some struggle. The only people to question were the spectators, and after much inquiry and climbing, I was lucky enough to find my seat. It had not been occupied, and there were then many vacant seats in that immediate neighbourhood.

Then the King arrived, and surely no Monarch has ever before been greeted by such a wild burst of cheering from such a throng. It was so marvellously impressive in its intensity that, stupidly, I wished his Majesty might be in that spot to hear it. No doubt the roar of sound was even more deafening round the Royal box.

For forty minutes what looked like a comparatively small body of police with about a dozen mounted men struggled rather aimlessly with an elusive crowd of thousands. At last order was restored and the ground cleared, but in that process great numbers of those pushed off the turf or standing in back rows from which they could see nothing of the game took advantage of the absence of any effective barriers to climb up the tiers of seats and occupy every vacant place within my view. Bolton supporters with rattles and rosettes were my immediate neighbours during the game. When it was over—but not till then—I was able to get out after much chair-climbing and struggling, and you will understand from my experience that the arrangements for dealing with a crowd of unexampled proportions with Cup-tie propensities were very thorough. I was never asked for my entrance or seat tickets, and have them still. They do not compensate me for what I lost in various tight places, but the vast assembly and the wonderful reception of the King were worth anything.

The first time I went to the Exhibition grounds I asked particularly about the means of getting there, as it seemed to me that was a matter of vital importance. I was told it would be a journey of seven or eight minutes from Baker-street or Marylebone to the ground. To-day I chose the Great Central, as it has a new "Exhibition" station. The journey there took thirty minutes; coming back I was pushed into what was probably the second train after the conclusion of the match. I saw four men fight their way into an over-full carriage of the first train. In my compartment of a third-class carriage we were twenty passengers. The journey to Marylebone took sixty-five minutes, five of them at rest in a tunnel, and I am sorry to say my fellow passengers agreed with the first remark of one of them, which was: "That's the last time I'll come here."

Many times on this return journey, when the train was standing still, my fellow travellers opened the door and shouted pleasantries to the engine-driver—"Has your coal run out, or have you only lost your way?" But the railway arrangements must have been admirable, too, for when the Cup Tie enthusiasts found themselves at Marylebone, many hundreds of them crowded to the locomotive and cheered the driver—derisively. Poor man, it was not his fault.

FRANK SWETTENHAM.

London, April 28.

INQUIRY DEMANDED INTO CUP FINA

Public Uneasiness Over Storming of Stadium by Uncontrolled Crowd of 100,000.

MANY WOMEN AND CHILDREN AMONG INJURED

The King's Intervention at Dangerous Moment—Disaster Averted by Tact of Police.

Not only by sportsmen, but by the general public, an official inquiry is demanded into the cause of the Cup Final debacle on Saturday at the new Wembley Stadium.

In the wild stampede, in which barriers were broken down and officials and police patrols swept aside by a seething, surging mass of 100,000 people, there were nearly a thousand casualties. It is marvellous that nobody was killed. Who was to blame for the organisation which was impotent to prevent over 200,000 men, women and children swarming into a place estimated to hold but 127,000 and literally taking possession of it?

This question not only the victims of the fiasco, but the public, for whom the Cup Final is a national festival, are entitled to have answered.

BARRIERS SWEPT AWAY BY HUMAN TORRENT

Impressions of One Who Was Jammed in Crowd.

CRACKING RIBS!

By SIR SIDNEY LOW.

I went to Wembley to see a great football match. I did not see a great football match, though I saw what, in the circumstances, much be considered a fairly good one.

But I saw some other things more interesting than the very best football.

I saw the crowd at the Stadium, and it was an unforgettable spectacle.

It has been my fortune to have looked at many huge crowds in several countries; but never in my life have I gazed upon so mighty a concourse of human beings congregated within a single enclosure.

INCREDIBLE SIGHT.

The throng, as you surveyed it from a reserved seat in the grand stand, was overwhelming, incredible, appalling in its magnitude.

The eye swept along the immense crescents, where the seats rose tier upon tier, with not one vacant space anywhere.

No benches were visible; only those heaps and layers of human faces, so squeezed together that clothes and hats were unnoticed, and the whole became one gigantic glow of pink, a concave mountain range of heads.

Down below on the level it was black, a mammoth dark swarm of pigmy figures, pushing and wriggling round the emerald oblong playing ground, and then pouring all over it in long columns or disorderly polygons, an army of ants or locusts, as they seemed to us from our heights.

From that comparatively secure elevation, once attained, one could survey the standing crowd in comfort. But to be in that crowd was a different matter, difficult, dangerous.

SWEPT INTO TORRENT.

I was swept into it on the way to my seat, caught by a dense and swirling stream, pushing towards the ring. I spent as awkward a ten minutes as I have had to endure.

The crowd was making for one of the iron enclosure gates which had been forced open.

One could not bear back or escape; there was nothing for it but to be carried along by this human avalanche, for there was the weight of five thousand bodies pressing it on from behind.

So close packed was this living mass that you ran no danger of falling and being trampled upon, but a quite appreciable risk of being squeezed to death.

A burly Lancashire man had his brawny elbows pressed close upon my right side—he could not have moved them if he had tried—and once or twice I felt my ribs cracking and wondered how long I could stand the strain.

My companion in this jam had a silver cigarette-case in his pocket, and it was crushed almost flat.

POLICE OUTNUMBERED.

I saw nothing for it but to allow myself to be carried right through into the ring. Fortunately, there was a little space between the open gate and the wall.

Into this, by a violent effort, I managed to slip, and there abode while the crowd steramed through, and so at length steered to my allotted place.

There I sat and watched the grim and splendid battle the police waged to clear the field, and keep it clear.

It was an heroic combat against impossible odds. Many of the constables were wearing war medals; I think they earned another bar to them on this fierce Saturday afternoon.

At first they were so utterly outnumbered as to be helpless. The foot police were whirled away like twigs in a Severn spate by that rush of thirty thousand men flinging themselves over and through the barriers.

There were about half a score mounted constables, and they did wonders, but of course were all too few.

When a horseman came prancing upon the intruders they retired a little before him, only to push forward again as soon as he rode to some other part of the line.

One officer on a white charger won the unstinted admiration of the "gallery," and was often and deservedly cheered.

Energetic, undaunted, resourceful, at once decisive and good-tempered, he dominated the crowd by the sheer force of his personality, and wherever he appeared he received willing obedience and made a little oasis of order in the general chaos.

But he could not be everywhere at once, and the temporary clearances he and his scanty band of comrades made, with the two football teams assisting, were soon submerged.

For an hour it looked as if it would be utterly impossible for the match to be played that day.

ANGRY NORTHERNERS.

Then, at long last, came the reinforcements. A whole squadron of mounted men rode upon the ground, and a strong company of foot police followed. A regiment and a battalion would not have been too many.

Slowly and with great effort the multitude was jostled and herded back just clear of the goal posts and lines, policemen sat down on the turf in front. So the game was played, as best it could be, with a seated policeman or too-prominent spectator having occasionally to be shifted for a corner kick and the ball frequently flying right into the depths of the serried ranks of onlookers.

My memories of the Cup final of 1923 will always be, first, the colossal throng which almost stunned the senses and left the imagination mute.

Secondly, the pluck, grit, tenacity and temper of the police.

GOOD-HUMOURED CROWD.

Scotland Yard may have mishandled the situation and withheld its reinforcements too long, but the conduct of the policemen and officers on the spot was beyond praise.

As for the crowd, though there was a good deal of violence, there was not, I think, any real viciousness.

Many of the rough Northerners were furious (and one could hardly blame them) at finding that they had come hundreds of miles and spent many hours and much money in order to reach an arena filled to bursting before they arrived.

But it was an English crowd with a riotous and rowdy element, but on the whole reasonable, kindly, good-humoured.

A thousand people or so were injured, but probably not one through malice or intention.

In any foreign capital the afternoon would hardly have passed without the throwing of stones, the flashing of steel and the snap of revolver shots.

But then is there any foreign police force or gendarmerie that could have kept its head and temper so well as the Metropolitan Police did through this ordeal? I think not.

OUR MESPOT BURDEN.

Sir Percy Cox: Perhaps British Will Leave in Four Years.

Perhaps in four years' time British responsibility in Iraq would end, said Sir Percy Cox, High Commissioner, speaking at a banquet in his honour at Bagdad.

Sir Percy added, says Reuter, that no doubt the British would stay till the country could stand alone.

The Iraq Premier told Sir Percy that his name would live for ever in the hearts of the people.

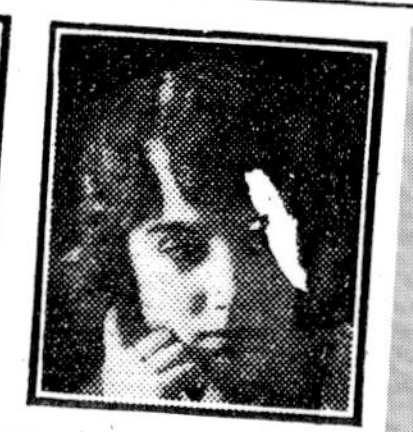

Mr. W. B. Leeds and his wife, Princess Zenia of Greece. Mr. Leeds is coming to England as an ordinary sailor, working on a freighter.

STADIUM'S MANGLED AND BROKEN GATES.

Iron Fences Twisted Like Indiarubber.

HOLE IN THE ROOF.

The authorities ran no risk of the Stadium being overrun by idle sightseers yesterday.

Every entrance and gap in the corrugated iron fence surrounding the ground was guarded by a strong force of police.

Outwardly, the Stadium shows no signs of having been carried by assault and battery.

There is a hole in the roof a little to the right of the royal box, where a too daring climber fell through on to a girder, but otherwise the damage consists of mangled and broken gates and wrought iron fences.

Many of these had been twisted into fantastic shapes, almost as though they had been made of indiarubber.

POLICE TRIBUTE TO CROWD.

One thing the crowd did respect—the refreshment bars. Thousands upon thousands scaled the turnstiles and barriers without paying, but it is recorded that everyone paid for his refreshment.

The arena itself, and the stands surrounding it, presented an unprecedented spectacle.

There has probably never been such a collection of debris in so small a compass—newspapers, paper-bags, empty bottles by the hundred thousand, pieces of mascots, men's overcoats and women's hats.

Many of the policemen on duty yesterday had been in the thick of Saturday's melee.

"It was something altogether outside my experience," one of them told *The Daily Mirror*. "The one thing that struck me was the amazing good nature of the crowd. They were always on good terms with us and perfectly friendly."

ORGANISATION'S FAILURE.

Escape from Calamity Probably Due to the King's Presence.

Gigantic in its proportions as is this Wembley Stadium—greater by far than the famous Coliseum at Rome—it was totally inadequate to accommodate the vast army of men and women who wanted to see the Final.

More than an hour before the game was timed to begin the gates were closed, but the crowds kept rolling up at the rate of a thousand per minute.

There were men who had been travelling all night from Yorkshire and Lancashire and other places in the North, and loud and angry were their protests when they found that the barricades had been forced, and that, although possessing tickets, they were unable to get into the ground.

Considering the size of the crowd and the pandemonium which followed the rushing of the turnstiles and let in a human avalanche, it seems miraculous that there was not a heavy loss of life.

The chaotic scenes will go down in football history as a most lamentable episode. The presence of the King, who presented the Cup and medals at the close of the game, probably averted a calamity.

EBACLE

F.A. CUP FINAL PHOTOGRAPHS: SCENES ON AND AROUND THE FIELD OF PLAY

The rival captains shaking hands before the start of play.

Butler putting the ball through for Bolton only to be given offside. Note crowd on goal line.

Moore, of West Ham, taking a pass from Ruffell.

Bolton appeal as West Ham get away with the ball.

The King (on right) presenting the medals. Smith, with the Cup, on left.

The King, accompanied by the Duke Devonshire, gazing on the amazing scene

Red Cross men attending to one of the many people injured.

A West Ham back effecting an energetic clearance.

A mascot cup for Bolton's charabanc.

SCENES AT THE FIRST

THE KING AT WEMBLEY.—His Majesty acknowledging the cheers of the vast crowd at the Stadium. The Duke of Devonshire is behind him.

TORMING THE STADIUM.—A section of the crowd swarming over the urnstiles. It is estimated that some eighty thousand people were outside the ground when the gates were officially closed.

THE AMAZING SCENE AT THE WEMBLEY CU Stadium, Wembley. The estimated accommodatic photograph, taken when the match should have be quarters of an hour late and was interrupted for t

CUP FINAL AT WEMBLEY.

—Extraordinary incidents marked the final tie of the Football Association Cup competition played for the first time at the Imperial
125,000 persons proved insufficient, and thousands of those excluded forced their way into the ground. This striking aerial
ess, shows how completely the crowd dominated the situation before police reinforcements arrived. The match, which was begun three-
by the crowd swarming over the touch-line again, was won by Bolton Wanderers, who beat West Ham United by two goals to none.

STANLEY MATTHEWS WINS FA CUP MEDAL AT WEMBLEY

CUP MEDAL FOR STAN—AT LAST

FOOTBALL maestro Stanley Matthews was on top of the world last night—proud owner at last of the F.A. Cup medal which had eluded him so long.

Stan Matthews Inspires Thrilling Cup Victory

BLACKPOOL GET TWO IN LAST 3 MINS.

MARVELLOUS STANLEY! KING OF FINEST FINAL OF ALL!

MAESTRO MATTHEWS!

Blackpool fight back to victory from 1-3 in most exciting-ever Cup Final

by ALAN HOBY

BLACKPOOL 4 (Hassall o.g., Mortensen 2, Perry) BOLTON 3 (Lofthouse, Moir, Bell)

SPORT PICTORIAL Page 3

PAGE 18 SUNDAY PICTORIAL, May 3, 1953

Grippled Bell is Bolton scorer

BLACKPOOL'S WHIRLWIND FINISH

PERRY SLAMS WINNER ★ STAN'S FINEST GAME

DONE IT!

PICTURE ANALYSIS . . . . . by ALAN HOBY

HERE he is — the amazing Wizard of Blackpool about to sell the dummy to Malcolm Barrass, the Bolton centre half — a master-move which led to the winning goal in the last minute of the match. Note Matthews's uncanny body balance, his extraordinary concentration, the way he never takes his eye off the ball even while executing Soccer's most intricate ballet-dance. Watching from the stand, I have never seen anything like it.

Oh! What a goal it was that won us the Cup

Blackpool have won the Cup. They went to Wembley yesterday for the third time in five years. They were one down in the second minute, but they won by a goal in the last 40 seconds. And here is the story—exclusive to the Sunday Express—told by the man who made the winning goal, the man all the world wanted to see wearing a Cup winner's medal. . . .

By STANLEY MATTHEWS

AS I struggled up the Wembley rostrum I was breathless and almost in a daze. At last! At last! Even then it was hard to realise that I had won my Cup Winner's medal.

I was proud at the terrific reception Blackpool got from the big crowd. I was happy not for myself but for my wife Betty, my mother, and the two children, up there in the crowd.

To them this honour meant so much. I was sorry too for the Bolton boys. After those earlier Manchester United and Newcastle defeats of Blackpool at Wembley, I know what it is like to lose.

My reactions as we went up for the medals—Blackpool first this time for a change—aren't hard to define.

I felt a sharp pang that Allan Brown and Hugh Kelly, out of the Final through injuries, were not to enjoy the full measure of our success.

That early Bolton shock goal gave me an awful feeling—just for a moment. Then I realised that if we could go on playing football we would win.

The turning point in the game was Stan Mortensen's terrific equaliser. He hit it like a rocket. I knew then that we would win, even if it went to extra time.

And then, that life-saving winning goal! Ewan Fenton twice lost the ball in a tackle with left-half Harold Hassall.

But he came through with it to set Ernie Taylor moving.

Ernie slipped me a lovely through ball and I beat Banks on the inside. As Mal Barrass came into the tackle I moved away to the wing.

Final move

Cutting in slightly before my centre, I had time to see Stanley Mortensen and Bill Perry working in to anticipate my final move.

The ball was a trifle wide for Morty, so, shrewdly, he left it to Bill Perry.

Mortensen had the situation sized up in a split second. He knew he could get to it but probably not score so he let my cross pass on to Perry and the left winger didn't make any mistake.

—AND LAST NIGHT

One hand gripping the Cup he helped so nobly to win, Stanley Matthews beams at the world at last night's banquet.

THE HAPPIEST MAN IN THE LAND

UP in the air for joy, on the shoulders of two of his team-mates, goes the happiest man in the land, after yesterday's Cup Final.

Yes—he is Stanley Matthews, and Stan has got **THAT MEDAL** at last. In the last half minute of the most exciting Cup Final ever seen at Wembley, Blackpool beat Bolton 4—3—after being 1—3 down in the second half.

Thrill followed thrill as the Blackpool men flung in attack after attack. Then Mortensen scored.

A couple of minutes before the end, Mortensen smashed home a third.

Forty-five seconds to go, and there began a movement that made the game the final of Wembley finals. Stan Matthews, playing superb football, raced forward, and Perry crowned his efforts with a whip-crack shot.

Blackpool—and Stan—had made it.

BLACKPOOL 4 (Hassall o.g., Mortensen 2, Perry) **BOLTON 3 (Lofthouse, Moir, Bell)**

IT is 22 minutes from the finish of this lurid, amazing, and utterly incredible Coronation Cup Final—easily the most exciting Wembley game I have ever seen.

Bolton Wanderers are leading 3—1, and the day seems black for Blackpool. Then the miracle happens.

Alone on the Blackpool right wing lurks the old Sorcerer of Soccer himself—that man with the giant gifts, that demi-god in football boots whose unique body swerve and dead-pan features are as dear to the nation as Sir Winston Churchill's cigar . . . Stanley Matthews.

Suddenly the ball is whipped out to him by little Ernie Taylor, Blackpool's inside right with the size four boots, and like a stalking cat the 38-year-old Wizard pounces.

A waggle and the crowd's roar—the roar which for 21 years the greatest ball juggler of all time has aroused time and again in hundreds of thousands of spectators — swirls and eddies above the vast grey bowl.

Another waggle and Ralph Banks, the Bolton left back, is fumbling and groping like a man who has just come out of a dark place into the blinding light of the sun.

Shufflin' Stan is through. The road to the Bolton goal—and victory (although we didn't know it at the time)—is open.

ASTONISHING

With that astonishing acceleration Matthews runs on before sweeping over a glorious centre to the far post.

Stanley Hanson, the Bolton goalkeeper, goes up to the looping, curling ball, but it is like a fish in his fingers and spirals down.

Then, with the whole of Wembley aflame, Stanley Mortensen—who has played his heart out—slides on to one knee and somehow pushes the ball into the net.

Another tremendous scream from the terraces and it's 3—2. Those Cup winners' medals for Stanley and Blackpool are not yet lost.

Now it is all Matthews, England's most beloved footballer and the world's No. 1 Soccer entertainer. He bewilders. He bewitches. He baffles that wildly kicking Bolton defence until they are in a panic plus.

THE NIGHTMARE

I've never seen anything quite like it. One man is winning the match for Blackpool—one man alone, the Master.

But Blackpool, with the nightmare of those two earlier Wembley failures in 1948 and 1951 very much alive in their memories, are still a goal behind.

Then, two minutes 40 seconds from the finish, after time had been added on by referee Griffiths for earlier hold-ups through injuries, little Jackie Mudie, the Blackpool inside left, is fouled just outside the Bolton goal area.

Barrass, the Bolton centre half, and Wheeler, their right half, both go to the tackle and bring down the Scot.

an hitherto undistinguished performance by hitting the ball along the turf and into the net.

4—3. . . Blackpool have won. And Wembley is in the grip of pure hysteria—and relief.

Yes, this final will go into history as "Matthews' Match."

Indeed, after all his magnificent services as an ambassador of sport and of his country it would be a fitting gesture in this Coronation year if this modest, unassuming star—the perfect gentleman both on and off the field—was given the knightly accolade of "Sir Stanley." . . .

In the first half Blackpool were paralysed when, after one and a half minutes George Farm, their Scottish international goalkeeper, allowed a speculative 25-yard Nat Lofthouse shot from the right to go off his arm and a post into the net.

JITTERS

It was a satin-soft goal, and a plain attack of jitters by Mr. Farm.

George, indeed, had a most unhappy game and for a long time Bolton, without playing brilliant football, had Blackpool on the run with nice moving attacks down the right.

Willy Moir, Bolton's captain, was slipping Blackpool's young reserve left-half, the raw and inexperienced Cyril Robinson, much as he liked.

As a result left-back Tommy Garrett, who broke his nose only last Saturday, was often left on his own to tackle the dual problem of Moir and Bolton's clever outside right, Doug Holden.

When Blackpool did attack their finishing was weak and hesitant, and it was an "own goal" by Harold Hassall which put them level.

Mortensen shot, the ball was going well wide when Hassall diverted it into the net. He held his head in horror when he saw what he had done.

CANNON SHOT

A free kick. Stanley Mortensen is running up to take it. There he goes—a cannon shot and, with the huge crowd paralysed into silence by the swiftness of it all, the ball is lodged in the back of the net.

The Blackpool players in their tangerine shirts are dancing and jumping, delirious with joy. A madly exultant, cavorting tribal group standing out from the rich green of the turf.

The score is 3—3. The game has been saved from the very jaws of disaster.

Enter THAT MAN. There is, of course, no one quite like Stanley Matthews. Professor of Witchcraft and honorary member of the Magicians' Circle (or, at least, if he isn't he should be.)

It is now 40 seconds from the finish of this magnificent and unbelievable melodrama. There we are, our hearts in our mouths (if I may dredge up a cliche) standing up on our feet and—yes, I'll admit it freely—bawling at the top of our voices. Pressmen who are supposed to be impartial and public alike.

For the Prince of Footballers, the King of Dribblers, that deceptively frail looking and slightly stooped shouldered figure down there on the manicured Wembley turf is again waltzing down the wing.

This time he shimmies for a split second like a Hawaiian hulu, hulu dancer. In front of him, as nervous as a covey of giggling girls, is the harassed, hapless Bolton defence.

PURE MAGIC

But don't blame them. No one in this moment of pure magic could stop Matthews. He is a wraith, a ghost, a phantom.

He slides inside one man. He moves outside another. He cuts in, cuts out. He is there He is not there.

Then suddenly he is round the whole of that packed Bolton defence right on the by-line, gliding in with the Bolton goalmouth gaping like an insomnia sufferer's yawn.

With as much coolness as you please, Stanley slips the ball squarely and easily across the goal where Bill Perry, the Blackpool left winger, redeems

TWO BLOWS

Previously Bolton had suffered two heart blows.

(1) Eric Bell, their left half, pulled a muscle and limped off to outside left, Hassall falling back to left half and Langton moving to inside left.

(2) Lofthouse, in the 19th minute, hit the post with Farm clawing helplessly. The ball rebounded to Langton, who shot, only for Shimwell to smother it practically on the line with Farm sprawling on the grass.

Six minutes before half-time Langton, who had worked his way over to the right, crossed a dangerous ball, which Farm nevertheless seemed to have covered.

But as the Blackpool goalkeeper ran out of goal to pluck it from the air Willy Moir, the Bolton captain, went up with him and the ball, as he said afterwards, glanced off him into the net.

Another goal for Bolton which was as soft as a satin quilt. Another terrible case of jitters by poor George Farm.

And so to that fantastic second half, with Bolton 2—1 up. Blackpool's Cup bid seemed ended when, ten minutes after half-time, Holden crossed a beauty from the right and Bell the cripple went up like a soaring gull with a broken wing to head home. 3—1.

HALO FOR HARRY

The rest you know.

But I must hand a Hoby halo to Harry Johnston, the Blackpool centre half. Johnston for most of the match corked Lofthouse, footballer of the year, like a fly in a bottle.

For Bolton, Hassall was outstanding with Moir, Holden, and Wheeler.

But my last few words are about the old maestro, now 38 years of age. As I was staggering out of the Pressbox afterwards, still dazed and mentally and physically exhausted by that blood-raising finish, I passed Joe Davis.

As one world champion paying tribute to another Joe, the snooker king, said quite simply: "Alan, I have never seen anything like it. How, oh! how can they keep a man like Matthews out of the England team? He is the greatest of them all."

BLACKPOOL : Farm ; Shimwell, Garrett ; Fenton, Johnston, Robinson ; Matthews, Taylor, Mortensen, Mudie, Perry.

BOLTON WANDERERS : Hanson ; Ball, Banks R. ; Wheeler, Barrass, Bell ; Holden, Moir, Lofthouse, Hassall, Langton.

Referee : Mr. B. M. Griffiths (Newport).

Quotes

as told to
JAMES CONNOLLY

● **STAN MORTENSEN** (the Blackpool centre forward): When I was taking the free kick before that equaliser, Ernie Taylor whispered: "I don't think there's room for shot."

But I saw a slight gap near the post and smacked it there with everything I had. And, boy! was I happy when it went in. I knew that as soon as I hit it that it was a goal.

● **HARRY JOHNSTON** *(Blackpool's captain): It's wonderful. I think we deserved to win, even if we did leave it rather late.*

● **BILL PERRY** (the Blackpool left-winger): I feel fine. I can't tell you what a thrill it was to score a winning goal at Wembley. Matthews made it with one of his typical square crosses and Mortensen left the ball to me.

● **BILL RIDDING** (Bolton manager). I'm disappointed and, after all, what manager wouldn't be. Yet I am glad for Stanley Matthews. What a marvellous player. He deserves this last great honour.

● **GEORGE FARM** *(the Blackpool goalkeeper): It was sheer bad goalkeeping. I was dead worried—not for myself, but because the lads tried so hard and I felt I was letting them down.*

At half-time I felt I was making a mess of everything, and confess that I was playing like an old woman. But everything came out right in the end, and that makes me more than a little happy.

● **ERIC BELL** (the Bolton left half): I chased Mortensen as he went through early in the game . . . then I felt my leg muscle go. I knew I was more or less out of the game.

Then, when Bill Holden's cross came over, I just went in and jumped to head the third goal. I didn't feel anything then, but, by golly! I did afterwards.

● **HAROLD HASSALL** *(the Bolton inside left): There wasn't much I could do about the Blackpool first equaliser. I saw "Morty" go past John Ball and tried to cut him out.*

He shot as I went in, and I felt the ball—although I didn't see it—glance off my toe into our own net.

● **BILL MOIR** (the Bolton captain): The boys gave every ounce that they had to give. It was just too much. Several had stomach cramp. I heard the Queen in a daze, and thought she said "Hard luck . . . a great game."

● **REFEREE B. M. GRIFFITHS** *(Newport): On my stop watch I made it exactly the 45th minute of the second half when Blackpool scored the winning goal. I had added on two and a half minutes for injuries in the second half.*

FINALE TO A GREAT FINAL

The picture everyone has been waiting to see—Stanley Matthews with his hand on the F.A. Cup (above), as with Blackpool captain, Harry Johnston, he is chaired from the Wembley arena by jubilant team-mates. And, below: Johnston receiving the trophy from the smiling Queen. Also in the picture is Sir Stanley Rous, secretary of the F.A.

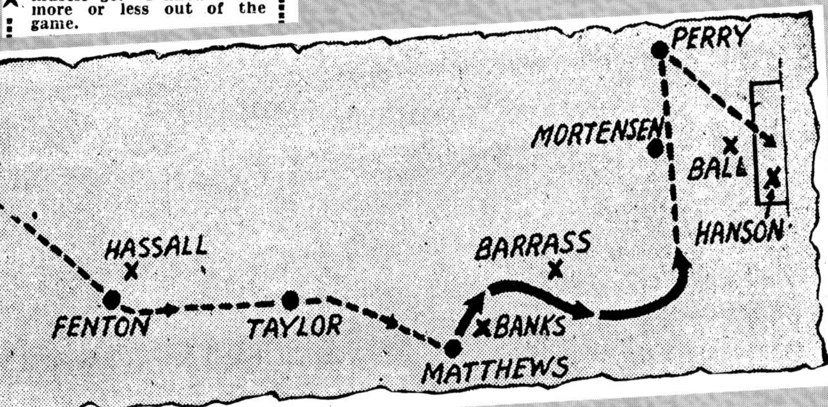

'BUSBY BABES' PERISH IN MUNICH AIR DISASTER

21 DEAD

MANCHESTER UTD PLAYERS PERISH IN AIR CRASH

SEVEN of "Busby's Babes," the best-known football team in Britain, died yesterday in the twisted wreckage of their chartered airliner.

Manchester United's Elizabethan airliner crashed at 3.4 p.m. while trying to take off in a snowstorm at Munich.

Of the 44 passengers and crew aboard, 20 died in the crash.

Another victim—Frank Swift, former England and Manchester City goalkeeper—died later in hospital.

Among the dead were well-known British sports writers returning with the team from Belgrade where United had drawn with the Red Star team and qualified for the semi-final of the European Cup for the second year running.

THE HORROR

Where the soccer stars died . . . a German policeman, revolver at hip, peers into the airliner's passenger cabin.

SAVED

Matt Busby *Manager*
Critical chest injuries.

Harry Gregg *Goal-keeper*
Minor head wounds.

Ray Wood *Goal-keeper*
Bruises, flesh wounds.

Billy Foulkes *Right-back*
Minor head injuries.

Jackie Blanchflower
Centre-half
Fractures, internal injuries.

Bobby Charlton *Inside-right*
Slight head injuries.

Dennis Viollet *Inside-left*
Shock, head injuries.

Johnny Berry *Outside-right*
Shock, concussion.

Ken Morgans *Outside-left*
Broken ribs, right leg.

Duncan Edwards
Left-half

Albert Scanlon
Outside-left
Shock, head injuries.

Skipper is a victim

The seven "Babes" who died included team captain **Roger Byrne,** 26-year-old English international left-back.

The other six were: right-half **Eddie Colman,** aged 21; centre-half **Mark Jones,** 23; centre-forward **Tommy Taylor,** 25; inside-forward **Billy Whelan,** 24; outside-left **David Pegg,** 22; and left-back **Geoff Bent,** 19.

Taylor also played for England. Whelan was an Eire international.

Tom Curry, United's trainer, **Bert Whalley,** the team coach, **Mr. W. Crickmer,** the team secretary, and **Mr. W. Satinoff,** Manchester businessman and race-horse owner who expected to join the club board, were also killed.

Manager Matt Busby is ill with chest injuries in a Munich hospital. A doctor said early to-day: "He has little chance. His condition is worsening."

Also injured and in hospital are star players Bobby Charlton, Jackie Blanchflower, John Berry, Duncan Edwards, Ken Morgans, Albert Scanlon, Dennis Viollet and Ray Wood.

Two other players, English international Bill Foulkes and United's new £23,000 goalkeeper Harry Gregg, were allowed out

SEVEN SOCCER STARS DIE

From Page 1

after treatment. Irish international Blanchflower has complicated fractures of the arm, broken ribs, a fractured pelvis and internal injuries.

Eight of Britain's best-known sports writers—Frank Swift was on the News of the World—died in the wrecked plane.

They were **Alf Clarke** (Manchester Evening Chronicle), **Tom Jackson** (Manchester Evening News), **George Followes** (Daily Herald), **Archie Ledbrooke** (Daily Mirror), **Henry Rose** (Daily Express), **Eric Thompson** (Daily Mail), and **H. D. Davies** (Manchester Guardian).

Frank Taylor, of the News Chronicle, was dragged from the wreckage. Early to-day he was seriously ill

Two other newspapermen—Peter Howard and Ted Ellyard, both Daily Mail cameramen — escaped unhurt.

Mr. S. P. Miklos, the travel agent who arranged the chartered trip, was also killed. His wife is in hospital.

Only one member of the BEA crew of six—steward W. T. Cable, of Farnham Common, Bucks—died.

The 37-year-old pilot, Captain James Thain, of London, escaped with slight injuries.

So did the two stewardesses—Miss Margaret Bellis, aged 37, from Whitley Bay, Northumberland and 24-year-old Rosemary Cheverton, of Paignton.

First-officer, Captain K. G. Rayment, of Billingshurst, is seriously injured. Radio operator George Rodgers, of Harlington, Middlesex, is also injured.

Also aboard and injured were Mrs. Vera Lukic, 24-year-old wife of the Yugoslav air attaché in London, and her 22-month-old daughter Venena. Yugoslav diplomat Mr. Thomasavich also escaped.

A BEA Viscount airliner flew BEA senior officials and accident experts to Munich three hours after the news of the crash reached London. On the plane was Mr. Anthony Milward, chief executive of BEA, who said:

"We know that the accident must have been caused by some sort of engine trouble."

The Elizabethans are in their eighth year of service.

Busby Babes' Elizabethan Down At Munich On Way Home From Belgrade

MANCHESTER UTD IN PLANE CRASH

Picture from yesterday's match in Belgrade. Bobby Charlton is scoring Manchester United's second goal.

AN AIRLINER CARRYING THE MANCHESTER UNITED FOOTBALL TEAM CRASHED AT MUNICH AIRPORT TODAY. BEA SAY SOME PASSENGERS WERE KILLED.

The plane plunged from 60 feet to the ground as it came in to land after flying from Belgrade, where the United drew yesterday with the Yugoslav side, Red Star.

A BEA spokesman said: "It is understood there were ten to 15 survivors out of 40 people on board. This is not definitely confirmed."

An unconfirmed report said the plane—a specially chartered BEA Elizabethan—was badly damaged, possibly a write-off.

Passengers Killed—10 to 15 Survivors

The Manchester United team in yesterday's European Cup match was: Gregg, Foulkes, Bryne, Colman, Jones, Edwards, Morgans, Charlton, Taylor, Viollet, Scanlon.

In the Manchester United team were a cluster of international players of countless price.

Gregg, Ireland's goalkeeper, they bought recently from Doncaster for a record sum for a goalkeeper.

Foulkes and Bryne, the full-backs, have both played for England, Byrne for more than four seasons.

Duncan Edwards, left half-back, had scarcely reached manhood, and yet was worth every bit of £40,000 to a home and probably £100,000 to an Italian club seeking such a star.

He played for England at the age of 18½, and set up a record thereby.

Tommy Taylor, England's centre-forward, cost the United £29,999 when they signed him from Barnsley four years ago.

The rest of the team was formed of Busby Babes, all found and nurtured in the manager's Old Trafford nursery.

The crash at Munich: at the top the aircraft lying in a field and: below, wooden houses on fire after being struck by burning wreckage

21 FEARED DEAD IN MUNICH CRASH

Matt Busby and 10 of his team survive

8 JOURNALISTS KILLED?

About twenty-one of the 44 passengers and crew of the British European Airways air liner which crashed yesterday near Munich, carrying the Manchester United football team and many journalists, are feared dead.

About eight others are in hospital, seriously injured. Frank Swift, the former international goalkeeper, who had become a journalist, died in hospital. Late last night the following official casualty list was issued :

THE DEAD

Bert Whalley : Coach.
Tom Curry : Trainer.
Roger Byrne : English international left back and United captain.
Eddie Colman : Right half.
Mark Jones : Centre half.
Bill Whelan.
Frank Swift : "News of the World"; former English international and Manchester City goalkeeper.
H. D. Davies : "Manchester Guardian"; Mr Davies wrote under the name of "Old International."
Tom Jackson : "Manchester Evening News."
Henry Rose : Northern sports editor, "Daily Express."
Archie Ledbrooke : "Daily Mirror."
George Follows : "Daily Herald."
Eric Thompson : "Daily Mail."
B. P. Miklos : Travel agent.
W. T. Cable : Steward.

UNACCOUNTED FOR

Walter Crickmer : Secretary.
Tommy Taylor : English international centre forward.
Geoffrey Bent : Full-back.
David Pegg : Outside left.
Alf Clarke : "Evening Chronicle," Manchester.
Frank Taylor : Northern sports editor, "News Chronicle."
W. Satinoff : A director of several Manchester companies.

The five of the crew who survived and are in hospital are the pilot, Captain J. Thain, the First Officer, Captain K. G. Rayment, two stewardesses, Patricia Bellas and Ruth Cheverton, and Radio Officer G. W. Rodgers, 35, of Harlington, Middlesex.

A report from Associated Press said that the aircraft crashed onto a hut full of oil and petrol. It was the fire from this which did the greatest damage—which was to the centre of the aircraft. The plane itself did not explode.

THE SURVIVORS

Matt Busby : United's manager since 1945.
Harry Gregg : Irish international goalkeeper, aged 24.
Ray Wood : English international goalkeeper.
Billy Foulkes : English international right back.
Jackie Blanchflower : Irish international centre half.
Duncan Edwards : English international left half, aged 21.
Ken Morgans : Outside right, aged 19.
Bobby Charlton : Inside right.
Dennis Voillet : Inside left
Albert Scanlon : Outside left.
Johnny Berry : Outside right.
P. Howard : "Daily Mail"; photographer.
E. A. Ellyard : "Daily Mail"; mobile photography operator.

Manchester United : on the back row, left, are Edwards (survivor), Foulkes (survivor), Jones (not known), Wood (survivor), Colman and Pegg (both not not known) ; front row : Berry (survivor), Whelan, Byrne and Taylor (not known), and, right, Viollet (survivor). Inset are, left, Morgans (survivor) and, right, Scanlon (survivor)

AIR LINER HITS HOUSE

Broke into two parts

From Victor Zorza

MUNICH, FEBRUARY 6.

Bobby Charlton, one of the members of the Manchester United team, who is in hospital in Munich, together with some of the other survivors, has described here how the crash took place. He said that the aircraft tried to take off once and had even got as far as the end of the runway but there appeared to be something wrong and it came back.

All the passengers got out and went into the waiting-rooms, where they waited for some ten minutes. They were then told that whatever had been wrong had now been put right, and they got back into the aircraft, which then taxied to the runway and made another attempt to get off the ground. But just as it approached the airport boundary something went wrong again and it caught the edge of the house with its wing just outside the airport.

House on fire

The story is now taken up by one of the eye-witnesses, the driver of a German car, who saw the aircraft hit the house, then go up and down again in the air, coming to rest between two houses. Almost immediately, one of the houses, on which part of the tail had come to rest, was on fire. Another German eye-witness, a lorry driver, who happened to be standing at the back of his house when he heard the crash, ran towards the aircraft straight away; when he got there, after a few minutes, there was already a car which had come in from the road near by standing there and a child, who had been thrown out of the aircraft, apparently only slightly injured, was being carried to the car to be taken away.

An injured member of the crew had also got out, and was trying to pull one of the passengers out. The aircraft had broken into two parts. The right wing and the right part of the cock-pit were relatively undamaged, but the left wing was broken off at the point where the engine had been. The engine had been wrenched out of the body of the wing. People who had been thrown clear, and some who had by now been pulled out, were lying about on the snow.

Captain helps

It had been snowing at the time of the crash, and it was still snowing in the evening, after the rescue operations had been completed. The captain, who did not appear to be seriously injured, was helping with the rescue operations. He had explained to the rescuers that the co-pilot was jammed in the cockpit. It was necessary to saw through to him from underneath the aircraft, and to get him out in that way.

Ray Wood, of the Manchester United team, who is also in hospital here, asked that his wife in Manchester should be told that he was only slightly injured and that she was not to worry about him. Another slightly injured member of the team in the same hospital is Mr Morgans.

"THREE ATTEMPTS AT TAKE-OFF"

Disaster few seconds after third

Mr Peter Howard, a "Daily Mail" photographer, who was stated to be the only journalist aboard the aircraft in a condition to describe what happened, telephoned this description of the crash to Manchester last night, after going back into the wreckage to do what he could in the rescue attempt. As he talked, ambulance men were waiting to take him to hospital to be treated for shock.

"It was snowing when we landed at Munich. We went off for refreshments and then back to the aircraft to continue the flight. I was sitting in the front row of seats on the starboard side. When the pilot tried to take off there seemed to be some kind of slight fault with the engines. He stopped. Then he tried a second take-off. That did not seem satisfactory so he taxied back to the apron to get things checked up. It was on the third take-off that we crashed. I think we were about the end of the runway only a bit above the ground.

Seats crumble

"The plane suddenly appeared to be breaking up. Seats started to crumble up. Everything seemed to be falling to pieces. It was a rolling sensation and all sorts of stuff started coming down on top of us. There wasn't time to think. No one cried out. No one spoke—just a deadly silence for what could only have been seconds. I can't remember whether there was a bang or not. Everything stopped all at once. I was so dazed I just scrambled about. Then I found a hole in the wreckage and crawled out on hands and knees.

"I turned and saw Harry Gregg, the goalkeeper. Gregg, Ted Ellyyard, the two stewardesses, the radio officer, and myself went back into the wreckage. I saw Captain Thain, one of the crew, start putting out small fires with an extinguisher. burst into flames but the fuselage did not catch fire."

Snow falling

Reuter and British United Press messages state:

The chartered twin-engined Elizabethan air liner crashed on the village of Kirchtrudering a few mintes after taking off in snow from Riem Airport at Munich.

It lost height almost immediately after leaving the ground and grazed a group of trees at the western end of the airport. At a height of only about seven feet from the ground it ploughed into a two-storey house, where the owner of a transport business had his home and offices. It was believed that no one in the house was killed or injured.

The tail of the aircraft broke off and burning debris was scattered for about three hundred yards around, setting several other houses on fire. The aircraft and the house into which it crashed went up in flames.

The aircraft came to rest on an even keel with both engines ripped out. The nose in front of the pilot's cockpit was badly damaged, but the pilot's cockpit itself looked among the least affected part. The aircraft had apparently partly burnt out in the centre section, and the wings were torn off outside the two engine mountings.

The eye-witnesses said that six of the injured were able to crawl away by themselves. Others were pulled from the burning wreck by rescue teams. All the available fire brigades in Munich went to the spot, and a large number of police were driven to the airport in squad cars.

Directly news of the crash was received, a British consular official went to the airport. Another consular official went to a hospital to which the injured were taken.

One report said that four children

SYMPATHY FROM THE QUEEN

And Marshal Tito

Football enthusiasts and others, throughout Europe, were stunned by the news of the Manchester United air crash. Among the expressions of sympathy were messages from the Queen to the Minister of Transport, Mr Watkinson, and the Lord Mayor of Manchester, Alderman L. Lever, M.P., and from Marshal Tito to Mr Macmillan.

The Queen's telegram to Alderman Lever said: "My husband and I have learned with great regret of the tragedy which will have caused so much grief to the citizens of Manchester." The Lord Mayor replied thanking them on behalf of Manchester "for their kind message of sympathy, which is deeply appreciated and which will give so much comfort and strength to all concerned."

The official Yugoslav news agency reported that Marshal Tito said: "I am deeply moved by the news of the disaster, which has severely struck British sport and the English people. I express my profound condolences."

Alderman Lever also received messages of sympathy from the German Consul in Liverpool, the Southern Football League, and Sir Jocelyn Lucas, chairman of the British Sportsmen's Club. Sir Stanley Rous, secretary of the F.A., who was in Edinburgh, immediately cancelled his engagements to return to London on hearing of the crash. "What can I say except that I am absolutely shocked at the news," he commented.

In England, all the M.P.s for Manchester constituencies were appalled. A message of profound sympathy was sent jointly last night to the Manchester United Football Club by the M.P.s for Manchester, Salford, Eccles, Stretford, Westhoughton, and Ashton-under-Lyne. The M.P. for Stoke South, Mr Ellis Smith, whose home is at Eccles and who is a passionate supporter of United, also signed the message.

Nation grieved

The Lord Mayors of Manchester and Birmingham and the Mayors of Salford and Stretford expressed their sympathy. Alderman Lever said the "whole nation" would be grieved to hear the news. Manchester United had been "ambassadors of British sportsmanship," he said. "Manchester is indeed a city of mourning to-night." Alderman Lever cancelled his public engagements for last night.

The board of directors of Wolverhampton F.C., whose team was due to meet Manchester United at Old Trafford to-morrow, issued a statement saying: "This catastrophe causes a loss which will be felt by those interested in Association football the world over."

Commenting on the loss of journalists who were on the plane, Mr J. G. Orange, past chairman of the Football Writers' Association and a management committee member, said: "The association has suffered a grievous blow by the tragic loss of several of its members."

BILLY WRIGHT BECOMES WORLD'S FIRST PLAYER TO WIN 100 CAPS

Wolverhampton salutes Billy Wright

100 CAPS TODAY

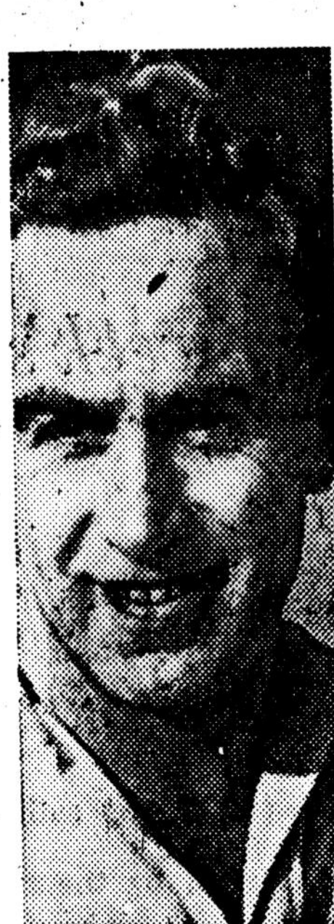

"Wembley: You must be getting to know the place," said Prince Philip to the Peter Pan of football...

THIS afternoon, around ten minutes to three, Billy Wright will pick up a brand-new football, loo round the Wembley dressing-room, remark: "Come on, lads, let's go out and beat them," then lea the England football team up that familiar sloping tunnel, from gloom to light, and out into th Wembley Roar. Ninety-nine times previously has Billy made that short walk in England's football kit fron dressing-room to international pitch all over the globe.

Today the football world salutes England's captain as he becomes the first-ever man to play 100 full international matches for his country.

Without a doubt Wembley is his favourite ground. So it is appropriate that on the lush green surface he gets the chance to top the hundred.

It has taken Wright nearly 13 years to run up this fantastic total. It was on September 28, 1946 that the fair-haired, solidly built boy from Ironbridge gained his first England cap at Windsor Park, Belfast, against Northern Ireland.

Leggat leads the Scottish threat

SPORTING TYPES by JON

BILLY WRIGHT'S 100th CAP

". . . and I'll bet it's the ...me size as the first"

TASK LOOKS TOO TOUGH FOR ENGLAND TODAY

IT'S a hundred pities . . . but I just can't see England giving Billy Wright at Wembley today the finest centenary present he could wish for—a victory over the Scots.

By JOHN CAMKIN

The English players are confident enough. But a study of the good and not-so-good points in both sides points to a narrow balance in favour of Scotland—who haven't won at Wembley since 1951.

And it's an Anglo-Scot who swings the balance. I mean Graham Leggat, frail but brilliant Fulham outside-right. Leggat's speed, plus his ability to move either inside or outside the full-back, may be too big a problem for young Sheffield United defender Graham Shaw.

I expect the Fulham flyer to supply a constant stream of passes to the heads of David Herd and John Dick, the two tall Scotland inside-forwards. With clever Bobby Collins at inside-right, Scotland appear to have the more threatening attack

Gamble

England's forward line is a gamble, for the selection committee has reverted to three ball-playing inside-forwards—Johnny Haynes, Bobby Charlton and Peter Broadbent.

Team manager Walter Winterbottom has faith in this formation. It has shown promise in practice this week at Arsenal and Chelsea . . as it did before the mud-ruined 3—3 draw against Ireland in Belfast last October.

Bobby Evans, the Scotland centre-half, hasn't always looked sure against fluid forward play. But today he is supported by Tommy Docherty and Dave Mackay, a pair of hard-tackling, quick-covering wing-half-backs.

Missed!

If England lose today a draw between Ireland and Wales in Belfast on April 22 would leave England and Wales holding the wooden spoon in the international championship. And Scotland would win the title outright.

In the main I expect a defensive game today, with England's Ron Clayton playing deep to mark Dick, the new Scottish cap.

IT COULD BE A DRAW TODAY. BUT THAT'S THE MOST I EXPECT.

Meanwhile, it's business as usual for Wright. He will earn his 100th cap—a record that may never be equalled. But neither England nor Scotland will grasp this golden chance to honour him before 100,000 admiring fans.

I know there will be official tributes later. I know there will probably be presentations at tonight's banquet.

But at Wembley itself only the grey terraces — brightened by tartan—will rise to acclaim the outstanding footballer of England. So a great opportunity is lost.

For Soccer, I believe, would expect and enjoy a little pomp and ceremony to honour Billy Wright in his finest hour.

No fuss

England's captain spent the eve of his 100th international quietly. After training at Roehampton he was at a West End luncheon to help a distinguished panel of F.A. and League representatives nominate the first holder of the Billy Wright Hundred Trophy.

Afterwards he spent an hour at the F.A. offices in Lancaster Gate before visiting his wife, Joy Beverley, and six-day-old daughter in the London Clinic.

POUND-NOTE: Victoria Ann weighs 8lb. 3oz. now.

Thank you ALL of you

BEFORE every match I suffer from butterflies in the tummy. At Wembley today I expect that I shall be a bit more nervous than usual—until the game starts.

*I think it's only natural. I'm excited and proud about my 100th cap, and the game is a climax to a memorable week and the achievement of an ambition I've scarcely **dared dream** about.*

Last Sunday I became a father for the first time and my wife and I have had literally hundreds of telegrams congratulating us on the double event. Little Victoria Ann is an absolute picture.

Answering

Telegrams have arrived from Australia, Hungary, U.S.A., Germany and several other countries, from many Football League clubs and from a lot of old friends in football.

Joy and I hope to answer each one—when we have a little more time. We shall be writing for many, many, hours, but we shall enjoy it.

In the meantime I would like to say a sincere THANK YOU TO EVERYONE who has wished us well.

BILLY YOU ARE A WONDERFUL EXAMPLE

My dear Sports friend,

I'm delighted that I have the opportunity to congratulate you on your 100th cap.

Please receive my very best wishes and I wish that for long years to come you shall lead the British colours to victory.

But for that big achievement I know what hard work was needed. Because I not only know you from your fame but I played against you three times and can honestly state that you were and still are one of the biggest footballers I have ever played against.

Your terrific drive, enthusiasm, your initiative, your love for the sport brought you where you now are. Which not many players could achieve.

Therefore, your 100th cap should be an example for all the footballers in the world. And your example should prove to them that you can achieve the 100th cap but only if they are taking an example from the one and only Billy Wright.

With my full-hearted sportsman's greeting—I remain, **Ferenc Puskas.**

SPURS BECOME FIRST BRITISH TEAM TO WIN EUROPEAN CUP-WINNERS' CUP

GLORY, GLORY, HALLELUJAH!

Greaves, Dyson send Spurs marching on

From PETER LORENZO: Spurs 5, Atletico Madrid 1

ROTTERDAM, Wednesday.

THE long wait is over. Here at the magnificent Feyenoord Stadium tonight Spurs, the team who have set so many firsts in our Soccer standards, became the first British side to win a major European competition.

The European Cup-winners' Cup is yours, mine . . and Spurs. It belongs to Britain, won by a team of Englishmen, an Irishman, a Welshman and two Scots who thrillingly, magnificently, recaptured the spark of greatness that at one time looked to be ebbing away fast.

Only for one 20-minute spell after half-time were Spurs really challenged by the Spaniards.

For two-thirds of this game Spurs, watched by their wives, sweethearts, and nearly 4,000 of their fervent fans, looked what they have been for three years until these last few faltering weeks—Britain's No. 1 team.

Spurs have given me a treasury

TERRY DYSON
. . his greatest game

of golden memories, but this was their finest hour.

They triumphed on their greatest strength — swift, penetrative, imaginative flowing football, embracing the finest qualities of our British game.

It would be easy to underline the flying, fearless pace and skill of Cliff Jones, the inimitable goal-snatching craft of back-to-form Jimmy Greaves, the resilience of Maurice Norman and his fellow defenders, the unflappable calm and polish of Danny Blanchflower.

But this was a team triumph, as much for the off-field tactics of Bill Nicholson as for the on-field magnificence of his players.

But there were men who stood out.

Tonight, Terry Dyson, son of a jockey, who has never ranked with the gifted elite of this star-spangled team, scored two goals and was the architect of a third.

Delighted

He played, in the words of overjoyed club manager Bill Nicholson: "The best game of his life. I never thought he could play so well."

Spurs, even without the swashbuckling courage and fire of crippled Dave Mackay, won praise from delighted, appreciative Soccer judges from all over Europe.

There will be cynics who sneer that this is Europe's second-best competition. But a competition is only as good as the sides taking part in it . . and tonight Spurs could never be described as second best.

Classic goal of a classic match was Spurs' first after 16 minutes —scored by Greaves, of course.

It stemmed from a swoop from the wing by Cliff Jones. He controlled brilliantly a flicked pass by Bobby Smith, whipped over a perfect cross.

And Greaves, of course, was there to flash a right-foot shot into the net.

Nineteen minutes later another right-wing cross from Jones. This time little Dyson was lurking there to prod the ball back for **John White** to pick his spot.

Confident

Spurs were so much in control and so confident, it just didn't seem possible that from a cross from the unmarked Enrico Collar two minutes after half-time Jose Mendoza could crack in a shot that Ron Henry could cnly save by punching it out from under the bar.

From the spot **Collar** stroked the ball home.

Twice 'keeper **Bill Brown,** more by courageous luck than judgment, saved certain goals.

Then, in the 67th minute **Dyson** scored . . the turning point of the match . . with a freak shot that drifted over the outstretched hands of the goalkeeper and it was 3-1.

Eleven minutes later **Dyson** swung over the pass for Greaves to make it 4-1 and three minutes from time, to crown the greatest match of his life, little Terry cracked in a solo fifth goal after running 40 yards.

My last picture of this wonderful night is of tough-guy Dave Mackay, the injured Scot who has given so much to Spurs in their three years of greatness, on the touchline weeping . . tears of joy, of course.

● It's there! Misery again for Atletico as the third goal flashes in.

● It's there! Jimmy Greaves, the man with the master touch, smashes super Spurs into the lead in the 16th minute.

● It's there! Atletico goalkeeper Madinabeytia claws the air as John White's shot nestles in the net. It's the 35th minute.

TRIUMPH IN ROTTERDAM—AS THE MEN FROM WHITE HART-LANE MAKE B

SPURS' 5-1 CUP

Blanchflower, chaired by Marchi and Smith, holds aloft the Cup of Cups. On left, Jones; on right, Baker.

Nicholson delighted

By ROY PESKETT

BILL NICHOLSON said after the match: "It was one of the finest Spurs have ever played. I'm delighted to be manager of the first England team to win a European tournament.

"Dyson was tremendous. We had to change tactics when Mackay was not playing.

"We started defensively with both wingers wide and Greaves behind them. We had to try to free him—and it worked well because he scored the first goal."

FRED WALE, Spurs chairman, said: "This must be the greatest performance of all time by Spurs. We started out a little despondent without Mackay, but the way the team played was a revelation."

☆

DYSON said of that last goal: "Bobby Smith was screaming for the ball, and I was going to pass to him until I saw the goalkeeper move. Then I shot into the top of the net."

Greaves said: "I was delighted with my right foot that sent the ball in for the first goal."

Atletico centre-forward Chuzo said: "No complaints. Spurs were good, although they played a hard game."

Atletico official Senor Melchor said: "Spurs would have defeated Benfica on this form. It was the best English side we've seen for years."

Dutch referee LEEUWEN singled out Norman, Dyson and Jones of a "superb" side.

SOCCER HISTORY

GLORY

The Greaves style (or just one of his many); he kicks goal No. 4.

HOPES ARE HIGH FOR ENGLAND'S 1966 WORLD CUP CAMPAIGN

Ramsey says it again: 'I'm certain of success'

ENGLAND TO WIN!

ALF RAMSEY dropped his bland mask yesterday and came out forecasting boldly: "England are going to win the World Cup."

He told world reporters in London: "I've been saying it since my appointment three years ago, and I say it again. I am satisfied that, to the best of my ability, I've done what I set out to do.

"We have deficiencies—and one is finishing. But I would be more worried if we were not making so many chances."

And Alf's view on Wembley, where England will fight all their World Cup battles. "Harder and faster than in the normal season."

But the club managers of England don't share Ramsey's confidence. A special "People" poll yesterday revealed that only half of them expect England to lift the World Cup for the first time.

The rest of the managers split almost equally between tips for Italy and West Germany. And that's also the view of "The People" experts.

GORDON BANKS (Leicester City). Goalkeeper. Born in Sheffield. Quiet, resourceful, brave, unspectacular. England player since 1963.

RON SPRINGETT (Sheffield Wednesday). Londoner, developed by Queens Park Rangers. Excellent on the line. More caps than any English goalkeeper. His second World Cup.

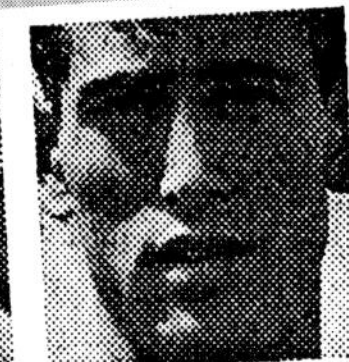

PETER BONETTI (Chelsea). Goalkeeper, from Worthing; supple and acrobatic in Continental style; ancestry is Swiss. Excellent debut in Copenhagen.

GEORGE COHEN (Fulham). A dedicated pro. Like Springett, born in Fulham. Two years an international, fast, strong, always ready to move into attack.

RAY WILSON (Everton). In his thirties, but playing with the exuberance of a teenager. Immensely quick on the ball, and in recovery. Comes from Mansfield.

JIMMY ARMFIELD (Blackpool). Right-back. Second World Cup. Thoughtful, mature player, who was born in Manchester, has had only one League club.

GERRY BYRNE (Liverpool). Converted from right- to left-back. Strongly-built player who has won Cup and League medals with Liverpool. First capped v. Scotland, 1963.

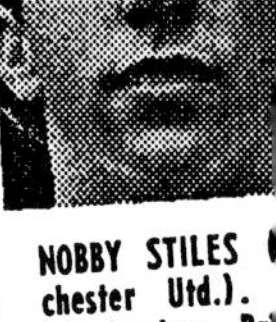

NOBBY STILES ... chester Utd.). ... but fearless. Bri... at Wembley as s... boy international ... half. Won full h... there in 1965 a... Scotland.

MARTIN PETERS (West Ham Utd.). Right-half, though can play almost anywhere. Dagenham born, enterprising, always keen to strike for goal.

JACKIE CHARLTON (Leeds Utd.). Centre-half. For years overshadowed by his younger brother Bobby, came into his own in 1964/65 with Leeds—then England.

RON FLOWERS (Wolves). Centre or left-half, though a wing-half by origin. Strong, straight-forward, in 1962 World Cup team.

BOBBY MOORE (West Ham Utd.). Captain of England. Tall, fair-haired, dominating half-back, fundamentally defensive, though he sometimes scores.

NORMAN HUNTER (Leeds Utd.). Left-half. Eager, active, first capped against Spain last year. Plays as cover to centre-half.

IAN CALLAGHAN (Liverpool). Outside-right. Enormously hard-working, intelligent, persistent. League and Cup medals with Liverpool, his only club.

JOHN CONNELLY (Manchester Utd.). Outside-right or left. From St Helens. Burnley developed him, been winning caps since 1958. Indefatigable, crisp, clever, quick.

TERRY PAINE (S... ampton). Outside-ri... Born Winches... helped Southam... win promotion to ... sion I last sea... Great success on ... first European tou...

● *Don't write off Uruguay because of those poor results during their tour of Israel, Rumania, Spain and Portugal. Says team boss Ondino Veira: "We didn't expect top form after the sudden change of diet and conditions.*

● *"But we're fully acclimatised now. My boys have never been fitter—physically or mentally."*

● *The Gay Caballeros make no secret about tomorrow's result. Their forecast: England 1, Uruguay 2.*

● *The man they most fear is Manchester United's Bobby Charlton. And Jimmy Greaves? "A good player, but he's the least of our worries."*

● *England players are on a £22,000 bonus if they win the World Cup. West Germany, who are fourth favourites, are on £2 a day spending money, plus ten stamped picture postcards of the Derbyshire Peak district.*

● *One London bookmaker reports having taken £37,000 in bets already, with a steady increase lately on West Germany and Italy.*

● *But one Italian fan has made a £1,200 bet . . . on England. Mexico and Switzerland are the outsiders at 200-1.*

Alf's method is OK—but he needs luck!

IF SPECTACULAR football is going to win the World Cup, rule out England.

If the prize is going to ball jugglers, goalmouth acrobats, midfield dancers, Alf Ramsey's team might just as well not come under starter's orders tomorrow.

For England are none of these things. England, as they made plain to half Europe on their recent tour, aren't even an entertaining side to watch.

But in this chilling age of concrete versus craft even Soccer artistry has lost its meaning. Only productivity counts.

And England, since Ramsey took over the team managership three year ago, have put results before appearances.

Outside these islands they have lost only once in Europe in that time. In the last 20 matches there has been just one defeat.

The latest away record, on the trip just finished reads, Played 4, Won 4, Goals For 12, Against 1.

Some of the England selectors were openly critical of the team's lack of crowd appeal, even after the Jimmy Greaves-inspired 6-1 win in Norway.

But they didn't mention this to Ramsey, their £90-a-week production manager.

Ramsey has always insisted: "Don't judge me now, judge me when the World Cup is over." And Ramsey has stuck to his ideas — and his rights.

For Ramsey, more than anyone, this is zero hour. His contract with England is running out. I don't think even Ramsey will ask for it to be renewed if we fail.

For Ramsey is a results man by nature. The supreme realist.

He insists: "We've as good a chance as anyone." And that confidence has spread to all the 22 players now under his command.

"I honestly believe we can win this damn thing," says that reformed pessimist Jimmy Greaves.

"We're *going* to win it," emphasises his skipper Bobby Moore.

Unspectacular

I didn't mention that Wilf Mannion had said the same thing to m before we set off for Rio n England's first World Cup tilt in 1950; that Stanley Mathews had said it before we wnt to Berne in '54. Tom Finne in Sweden in '58, and Johnny Haynes in Chile in 1962.

I only reied: "I wish you all luck." nd that includes Alf Ramsey

At this mnent I would feel more confint if England, fighting the battles on the retreat, coulonly *appear* to be in greater corol in midfield.

Ramsey, Ielieve, will open with his favrite 4-3-3 formation, hope, en pray, for an early goal a then revert to solid defencevith an unspectacular 4-4-2.

Greaves andunt will be left as England's le men up front.

"Bloody harwork," Greaves calls it, but en he doesn't complain of n having fire in his belly whe he plays for England now.

Perhaps tha is Ramsey's

An England win on the cards? Ron Springett checks on Bobby Charlton's hand.

TOMORROW'S LINE-UP

GORDON BANKS (Leics)
GEORGE COHEN (Fulham)
JACKIE CHARLTON (Leeds)
BOBBY MOORE (W. Ham)
RAY WILSON (Everton)
NOBBY STILES (Man. Utd.)
ALAN BALL (Blackpool)
BOBBY CHARLTON (Man. United)
JIMMY GREAVES (Spurs)
ROGER HUNT (Liverpool)
JOHN CONNELLY (Man. United)

World Cup winning secret—self-confidence and "bloody hard work."

I repeat, I wish them the best of luck. They should, they must, dispose of Uruguay at Wembley tomorrow. Mexico next Saturday shouldn't be a problem.

Alan Ball, perhaps the hardest worker of them all, was complaining after the Continental tour of an ankle injury which was "giving him hell," but which, he swore, would clear up in time for the big kick-off.

Jackie Charlton, had a knock, too. But last night's report from England's Hendon H.Q. was: "Casualties nil."

So Ramsey, who names his team today, will doubtless pick the squad shown above.

They, I think, will be his mainsprings—unless he prefers to run entirely on the defensive, when Peters will replace Connelly.

If you're going to Wembley, don't boo them for boring you. Just give them a big hand and wish them well.

Let this forecast from 80-year-old Vittorio Pozzo, the man who managed Italy in their two World Cup triumphs before the war, encourage you.

"I think the Cup will go to either Italy or Germany," I had told him.

"No, no," he said. "I think England. They're the super method team of 1966."

I take Italy's dazzlers

● *GERRY HITCHENS, Bergamo and former Inter-Milan and Torino centre-forward, concludes his exclusive World Cup series with this assessment:*

I'LL BE IN the crowd at Wembley tomorrow cheering hopefully for the white shirts of England.

Last World Cup I was wearing one—the number nine in Chile as the only Continental club player ever to represent England.

Since then I've stayed in Italy with Inter-Milan, Torino and Bergamo and reckon I know more than most Englishmen about foreign form.

So I say confidently that England will beat Uruguay tomorrow and Mexico next Saturday.

I believe Alf Ramsey's team will even beat World Cup holders Brazil if they meet in the competition. I'm not impressed by the bookies' prices for my information is that the favourites are over the top.

England have never been further than the quarter-finals of a World Cup. Sometimes we've not even got that far, but there's no doubt in my mind that we'll be in the last eight this year.

Desperation

England, France, West Germany, Spain, Brazil, Hungary, Italy, Russia—that's my idea of the quarter-final teams.

But I'm making no encouraging forecasts about England after the quarter final. For I wonder if they'll be good enough when the heat is on.

England's weakness is that when things go wrong there is too much desperation about their methods.

Too much hasty tackling, too much panic shooting.

The defensively minded Italians are saying: "If we meet England, we'll let them press and press. They're sure to make mistakes." I'm afraid they're right.

Most Continental sides—the Italians especially—will be content to let opponents make all the midfield running.

The order will be: "Let them get as far as the 18-yard line. They can't do much damage till then."

But, on that penalty box line, any raiders will come face to face with an almost impenetrable barrier that has always one defender to spare.

In Italy we call this spare man the "libero," in England you call him the "sweeper" . . . and his job will be done by Bobby Moore or Nobby Stiles.

He'll have to be cagey, challenging instead of tackling, cutting off instead of going in.

Far too often I've seen English defenders rush their tackles and finish up on their backsides while the opposition surge through. Watch it!

In this class of football, one slip, one fall, one defender off his feet for an instant can put a side out.

Final tip

England can play this defensive game, they've proved that by conceding only one goal in their last five matches.

They know, as all Continentals have known for years, that even the greatest forwards—Pele (Brazil), Suarez (Spain), Rivera (Italy)—can be shackled by playing a man on their toes right from the whistle.

But can English forwards succeed against the same trick? Are they good enough to get goals against the tightest marking ever seen on British football fields?

I'm sorry to say that I don't think they are. England's attack, even with Jimmy Greaves and Bobby Charlton, hasn't a world champion look

My opinion is that there'll be white shirts at Wembley for the final on July 30—but they'll be German not English.

And the opposing colour will be blue—Italy.

This would be a World Cup Final of steadiness against occasional brilliance, and dogged attack against massed defence.

There won't be much in it, but that little should favour Italy.

Yes, it's Italy, twice pre-war victors, to win the World Cup outright.

And I'll be delighted (won't we all?) if England prove me wrong.

The gaes . . . when and where

Games in the fi week of the World Cup are:

GROUP ONE.—Tomorrow: England v. Uruguay (Wembley, kick-off 7.30); Wnesday: France v. Mexico (Wembley, 7.30); Friday: Uruguay France (White City, 7.30); Saturday: Mexico v. England (Weny, 7.30).

GROUP TWO.—uesday: W. Germany v. Switzerland (Hillsborough, 7.30); Wesday: Spain v. Argentina (Villa Park, 7.30); Friday: Switzerla v. Spain (Hillsborough, 7.30); Saturday: Argentina v. W. many (Villa Park, 3.0).

GROUP THREE.—Tuesday: Bulgaria v. Brazil (Goodison Park, 7.30); Wednesday ungary v. Portugal (Old Trafford, 7.30); Friday: Brazil v. ngary (Goodison Park, 7.30); Saturday: Portugal v. Bulgar Old Trafford, 3.0).

GROUP FOUR.—sday: Russia v. North Korea (Ayresome Park, 7.30); Wednes Chile v. Italy (Roker Park, 7.30); Friday: North Korea v. Ch (Ayresome Park, 7.30); Saturday: Italy v. Russia (Roker Park).

ALAN BALL (Blackpool). Small, red-haired, dedicated player. Inside-forward, though Ramsey often uses him in No. 7 jersey. Valued at over £100,000.

GEORGE EASTHAM (Arsenal). Inside-forward. Skilful, deceptively fragile, highly intelligent midfield player. He began in Ireland, joined Arsenal 1961.

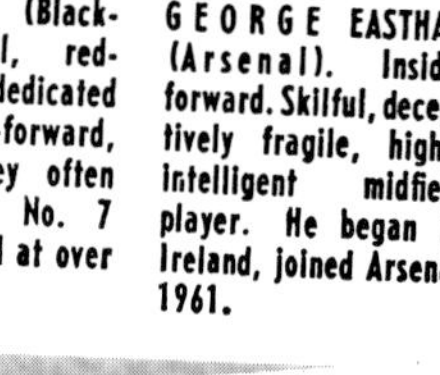

JIMMY GREAVES (Spurs). Inside-forward; one of the world's greatest strikers. A League star at 17, he holds the English international scoring record.

ROGER HUNT (Liverpool). A North-Easterner, Liverpool's chief striker, Cup and League medallist. In and out of England team till his recent lively improvement.

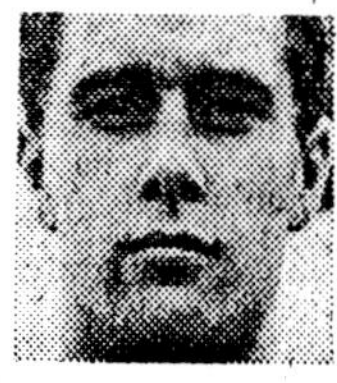

GEOFF HURST (West Ham Utd.). Striker. Powerful, courageous player who came into England's attack this year, after scoring heavily for West Ham.

BOBBY CHARLTON (Manchester Utd.). Plays anywhere but outside-right, second to Greaves as England's top scorer. Cup Final player at 17, major star at 18.

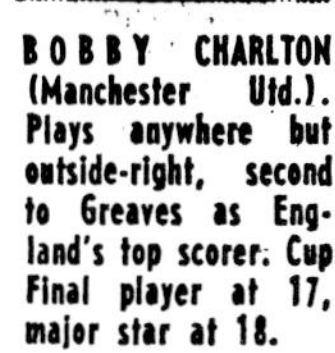

WORLD CUP '66: ENGLAND DRAW 0-0 WITH URUGUAY IN FIRST MATCH

Angry, baffled, goal-less

AND, AT THE END, ENGLAND WERE NOT ALL THERE!

England 0 Uruguay 0

Final National Anthem parade of Ball, Stiles, Wilson, Moore, Bobby Charlton, Cohen and Banks. Absentees: Jackie Charlton, Greaves, Hunt, Connelly.

The pattern typified: Greaves sets off for goal, pursued by Ubinas. Result: No score.

PROGRAMME

Remaining fixtures (kick-off 7.30 unless stated)

GROUP 1

Tomorrow—France v. Mexico (Wembley). July **15**—Uruguay v France (White City); **July 16**—England v Mexico (Wembley); **July 19**—Mexico v. Uruguay (Wembley, 4.30). **July 20**—England v. France (Wembley).

GROUP 2

Today—Switzerland v. W Germany (Hillsborough); **Tomorrow**—Argentina v. Spain (Villa Park). **July 15**—Spain v. Switzerland (Hillsborough). **July 16**— Argentina v. W Germany (Villa Park, 3.0); **July 19**—Argentina v. Switzer- land (Hillsborough); **July 20**—Spain v. W. Germany (Villa Park)

GROUP 3

Today—Brazil v. Bulgaria (Goodison); **Tomorrow**—Hungary v. Portugal (Old Traf- ford). **July 15**—Brazil v. Hungary (Goodi- son); **July 16**—Bulgaria v Portugal (Old Trafford, 3.0); **July 19**—Brazil v Portugal (Goodison); **July 20**—Bulgaria v. Hungary (Old Trafford).

GROUP 4

Today—N. Korea v. Russia (Middles- brough). **July 13**—Chile v. Italy (Sun- derland). **July 15**—Chile v. N. Korea (Middlesbrough). **July 16**—Italy v. Russia (Sunderland, 3.0). **July 19**—Italy v. N. Korea (Middlesbrough). **July 20**—Chile v Russïa (Sunderland)

QUARTER-FINALS

July 23 (3.0)—**Match A**—Winners Group 1 v. Runners-up Group 2 (Wem- bley). **Match B**—Winners Group 2 v. Runners-up Group 1 (Hillsborough). **Match C**—Winners Group 3 v Runners- up Group 4 (Goodison). **Match D**—Win- ners Group 4 v. Runners-up Group 3 (Sunderland).

SEMI-FINALS

July 25 (Goodison). **July 26** (Wem- bley)

Winners Match A v. winners Match C. Winners Match B v. winners Match D.

THIRD PLACE FINAL

July 28 (Wembley).

FINAL

July 30 (Wembley, 3.0). Replay, if necessary, **August 2** (Wembley).

GROUP ONE

	P	W	D	L	F	A	Pts
England	1	0	1	0	0	0	1
Uruguay	1	0	1	0	0	0	1
France	—	—	—	—	—	—	—
Mexico	—	—	—	—	—	—	—

'It was like tryin
...and not being

OH, ENG
A STAR

Match facts

THIS was the first time England had failed to score in 52 post-war internationals at Wembley. It also ended their run of seven successive wins.

GOAL ATTEMPTS

England 17 Uruguay 11

2 saved, 3 blocked 11 wide or high, 1 hit bar. — 1 saved, 3 blocked, 7 wide or high.

CORNERS

England 15 Uruguay 1

THROWS-IN

England 21 Uruguay 21

FOULS BY

England 16 Uruguay 18

OFFSIDE

England 0 Uruguay 1

GOAL-KICKS

England 10 Uruguay 23

QUOTES

We'll win —Ramsey

o pick the lock of a safe
e to find the combination'

AND, WHAT
T!

By
DESMOND HACKETT

England 0
Uruguay 0

At Wembley. Attendance: 75,000. Rec.: £85,000.

ENGLAND did not look the best team in the world, or in the World Cup, as they laboured endlessly against a light-blue brick wall of defence called Uruguay last night.

After the glory of the opening ceremonies the first commandment of the World Cup was written starkly across the noble turf of Wembley:

THOU SHALT NOT LOSE.

That was the creed and philosophy of Uruguay. It was a creed that permitted England only two shots demanding saves—and the first of these did not arrive until the 65th minute.

England could not be faulted for their effort or their courage But it was clear they had no notion as to how to get round a defence that was often eight and nine players deep.

Endless booing

The Uruguayans were booed endlessly for flagrant wasting of time. The swarthy, muscular champions of South America were unmoved and unhurried.

The England I most admired were in the stands. Never has Wembley resounded to such roaring encouragement as the splendid fans gave last night.

England's courageous first minutes charged the crowd with tremendous optimism, but slowly the Uruguayans took a hold of the game that was never relaxed.

Uruguay produced the only shot of the first half. It came after 27 minutes when husky outside right Julio Cortes rifled in a shot that brought out a World Cup-type save from Gordon Banks.

Jimmy Greaves, who seldom got on terms with the action, gave England their best chance with an accurate cross that was missed by four England players. And four England players up in the opposing penalty area was a rare luxury in this game.

As the England attacks rebounded harmlessly off the deep Uruguayan defence I began to feel sorry for manager Alf Ramsey.

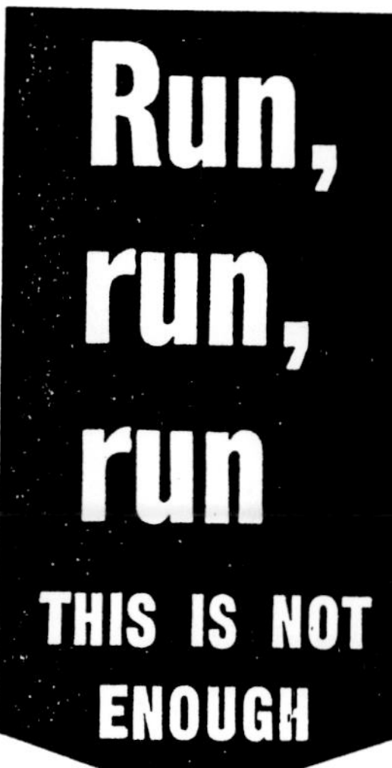
Run,
run,
run
THIS IS NOT
ENOUGH

By ERIC COOPER
Express Northern sports columnist

SHORTLY after the war I heard a schoolmaster call to his team: "Kick it boys, kick it hard and run."

I don't know what happened to the schoolmaster but he could well have been in charge of the white-shirted Englishmen who battled so hard to master Uruguay.

They didn't just kick the ball, and kick it hard. There were some good movements too. But they ran and ran and ran until I was left wondering how long the Lions of Lilleshall could keep on running in the 1966 World Cup Competition.

Team manager Alf Ramsey made it clear throughout England's training—at Lilleshall in pre-international get-togethers, and on the Scandinavian tour—that the accent was on physical fitness.

Was it also part of a Ramsey gamble that if England could not match foreign skills, they might still win through by strength and effort?

If so, the idea was rudely exposed by Uruguay, a team of skill and composure as well as power

England had their magnificents, such as gallant defenders George Cohen, Ray Wilson, and Jack Charlton.

Bobby Moore was a splendid captain, and Bobby Charlton, Alan Ball, and Roger Hunt must have run themselves dizzy in their efforts to cover every square yard of the pitch.

But Uruguay had just as much success without so much effort. And that could be a vital long-term factor in the games to come on the testing Wembey turf.

★

This dour Uruguay defence sets a disastrous pattern

By KEN JONES

URUGUAY dropped a defensive curtain on the World Cup last night as they held England to a goalless draw at Wembley.

They set the pattern for games to come, and have perhaps destroyed this championship as a festival of football before it had a chance really to get under way.

ENGLAND	**0**
URUGUAY	**0**
Att.: 75,000.	

All those dreams of fine and elegant competition died at Wembley.

This was the dourest of defensive battles that ended with the blue-shirted Uruguayans leaping in delight.

No doubt they regarded the result as a triumph, but the booing Wembley crowd looked at it as a disaster for the game.

Uruguay's powerful but skilful footballers soon troubled England when left winger Perez came in to meet a centre from the right with a powerful header.

Unfortunately for Perez, the chance was already ruled out, because he had moved into an offside position.

Any Distance, Every Angle

England swept into an early wave of pressure. But the South Americans, with forwards pulled back to reinforce their defence, and with Troche patrolling behind their back line, were difficult to break down.

They refused to allow England room in which to operate, and then marked tightly once they had consolidated their defensive deployment around their own penalty area.

When the Uruguayans set up their own attacks, they quickly got men up in support of Perez and centre forward Silva, and they were ready to shoot from any distance, and from every angle.

England's first move of real promise broke down, when Greaves tried to beat three men and Bobby Moore had to back-pedal furiously to reorganise a defence that had come forward to the half-way line.

The first shot to trouble the Uruguayans came when left winger John Connelly cut in to try a hopeful effort that went just over the top.

Moment of Hope

Then a foul on Roger Hunt brought England a moment of hope.

After Hunt himself had taken the free kick, the ball bobbed about in the goalmouth. And it was Hunt again who eventually had a fierce shot beaten down by Rocha.

In an attempt to force their way through, England pushed Connelly up on top of the Uruguayan "sweeper" Troche.

But the ball did not come through quickly enough, and the Uruguayans were always able to muster men quickly enough to smother England's attacks.

A little needle crept into the game, and Hungarian referee Istvan Zsolt ran quickly to speak to Uruguayan forward Viera after a bad foul on Bobby Charlton.

The next real flash of finishing power came from the Uruguayans when the skilful Cortes shot powerfully.

But he found goalkeeper Gordon Banks perfectly positioned to push the ball away for a corner-kick.

England still had trouble in winning possession from the South Americans who cleverly and courageously "screened" the ball away from some fierce tackling.

Another bad foul, this time by Silva on Alan Ball, brought the Uruguayan a telling off from Zsolt, and England were discovering that they had to fight for everything.

There was the promise of success when a Greaves free kick was pushed on by Moore to Bobby Charlton, just outside the penalty area.

The finishing shot was powerful, and almost accurate enough to beat goalkeeper Mazurkieviez.

Chopping 'Em Down

Hunt powered in to shoot over the top as England warmed again to the contest—and their challenge was met by men who were quite prepared to chop their opponents down on Wembley's turf.

Another foul, by Cortes on Ball, angered the Blackpool forward, and should have earned more than just the finger-waving admonishment of Zsolt.

It seemed at this stage as though England were suffering because of their over-awareness of the occasion—and of the presence of royalty in the stands.

They had to tackle harder to meet ruthlessness with ruthlessness, and they were not doing it.

Bobby Charlton shot powerfully over the top, and then at the other end Goncalvez sent a threatening shot wide of Banks.

The defensive trend that has always threatened to settle in on the championship was more than evident.

The Uruguayans continually reinforced their defence, and there was not one moment when England could get a man in for a clear strike at goal.

The match at the halfway stage had become hard work for all of England's players.

Clever covering by Moore got England out of trouble early in the second half when he headed clear from Rocha as the Uruguayan sprinted into an attacking position.

And when England mounted another attack centre half Jack Charlton was hurt as he went up to try to finish clever work by Stiles and Ball.

Greaves Slips Up

Greaves messed up a chance created by Bobby Charlton and then a sudden strike by the Uruguayans finished with Rocha volleying well wide.

In the sixty-fifth minute England created their first real chance.

The ball came out from a packed penalty area to Bobby Charlton and his fierce, first-time shot was deflected against the goalkeeper's chest by Connelly.

England now threw everything into attack, but their effort was not enough to break down the numerical strength and physical power of the Uruguayan defence.

There was no complaint at England's effort but there just wasn't enough alertness or instinctive understanding to find a way through a forest of defenders.

England attacked continually in the last fifteen minutes.

At long last they seemed to scent the right avenue of approach, sending Greaves and then Hunt pushing through on well-directed long passes that didn't give the Uruguayans time to mass their numbers in defence.

But still that vital goal eluded them.

ENGLAND—Banks, Cohen, Wilson, Stiles, J. Charlton, Moore (capt.), Ball, Greaves, R. Charlton, Hunt, Connelly.

URUGUAY.—Mazurkieviez, Troche (capt.), Manicera, Ubinas, Goncalvez, Caetano, Cortes, Viera, Silva, Rocha, Perez.

Referee: I. Zsolt (Hungary).

Linesmen: D. Roumentchey (Bulgaria), T. Bakhramov (U S S R).

OH! FOR FINNEY ON THE WING

By BILLY LIDDELL

LET'S not talk too much about England WINNING the World Cup. We ought to be more worried about whether they are going to qualify from their group.

For England did not click last night and the Uruguayans showed themselves to be a far better side than we expected.

I haven't seen either France or Mexico recently, but both these teams will have to be good to beat the South Americans.

It was halfway through the second half before England had a straightforward shot on the target, a good effort from Bobby Charlton, helped on by John Connelly, which goalkeeper Ladislao Mazurkieviez just scrambled away.

TOO DEEP

This was one of the rare occasions when Bobby Charlton came up. He plays too deep too much of the time.

England's running off the ball wasn't very imaginative. With such a big defence as this it was pointless lofting the ball into the middle, especially as Roger Hunt had a bad game.

More use should have been made of the wings. To beat this kind of defence you have to hit the ball hard across the middle, but it never came. Greaves was hardly seen and certainly didn't strike his deadly scoring form.

How England could have done with a Tom Finney out there to take that ball round the back and get it over.

That is the only way to break through these packed defences.

☆ ENGLAND'S display shook their World Cup odds. After the match Ladbrooke pushed England out to 6-1 (from 7-2) while William Hill made them 4-1 (from 3-1) and cut Uruguay from 40-1 to 16-1.

ngland's John Connelly (right) forces Uruguay to concede a corner as he challenges defenders Horacio Troche foreground), Nestor Goncalvez and goalkeeper Ladislao Mazurkieviez in the World Cup opener at Wembley last night.

Heads it's Jack— but raid fails

Desperate moment for Uruguay as Leeds United's Jack Charlton races upfield, soars above the South Americans' skipper, Troche, and tries a header at Wembley. But Charlton's effort, like so many of England's last night, was off target.

● RAY WILSON, England full-back, takes off in a dramatic airborne dive to head the ball away from Domingo Perez—and another Uruguay attack comes to nothing.

RAMSEY SNUBS BBC

ENGLAND team manager Alf Ramsey refused to be interviewed by the BBC after the match. He also refused an approach by Uruguayan FA president Conrado Saez to be allowed to visit the England dressing-room. Said Saez: "I am very disappointed about this."

Instead of using the interview room for Ramsey, the BBC used it for an Argentine broadcast. When it was over, the BBC asked Ramsey to be interviewed. Replied Ramsey: "No, I was available before and no one wanted me. Now it is too late."

Waiting journalists were told a duplicated interview would be issued instead. In this, Ramsey said: "I was disappointed with the result, but not with the performance. Uruguay were a good side. I felt before that they were tough and so it proved.

"Naturally I was disappointed we did not get a goal, but with seven or eight opposing players in the 18-yard box, you had to be lucky to get a break. . . . But I still believe we are able to win the World Cup."

In the Uruguayan dressing-room, team boss Ondino Viera said: "We were very happy with the draw."

WORLD CUP '66: ENGLAND BEAT MEXICO 2-0 TO ACHIEVE FIRST VICTORY

England's team that played Mexico at Wembley Stadium yesterday. Left to right, back row: George Cohen; Martin Peters; Gordon Banks; Nobby Stiles; Bobby Moore (captain). Front row, left to right: Jimmy Greaves; Jackie Charlton; Terry Paine; Ray Wilson; Roger Hunt; and Bobby Charlton.

ENGLAND SCORE GOALS WITHOUT GLORY!

QUOTES

ALF RAMSEY, England team manager: "I'm concerned about our finishing but there was never any doubt we would win. The players were over-anxious before the match. England have never been able yet to settle down and play the football they are capable of."

IGNACIO TRELLES, Mexican team manager: "The result was just. I congratulate England."

NO WORDS NEEDED

Roger Hunt has scored England's second goal. Bobby Charlton walks away while Mexican Pena expresses his grief.

GROUP ONE

	P	W	D	L	F	A	Pts
England	2	1	1	0	2	0	3
Uruguay	2	1	1	0	2	1	3
France	2	0	1	1	2	3	1
Mexico	2	0	1	1	1	3	1

GROUP TWO

	P	W	D	L	F	A
W. Germany	2	1	1	0	5	0
Argentina	2	1	1	0	2	1
Spain	2	1	0	1	3	3
Switzerland	2	0	0	2	1	7

BLIMEY, WE'VE

Now England are favourites for the Cup

England 2, Mexico 0 **By MAURICE SMITH**

ENGLAND look set for the World Cup quarter-finals.

For last night they showed that they have learned how to beat a blanket defence — by shooting on sight.

Forget that last time England and Mexico met at Wembley, the Mexicans were crushed 8—0.

Forget even that our man Greaves has still to score in this World Cup.

The important fact is that this new fighting, sleeves-rolled-up England are right in the mood.

The Mexicans tried to stop them with a defence packed tighter than a rush-hour bus.

Yet England had the answer. Yes, it was to shoot on sight.

And to do our hearts even more good there was stalwart Jackie Charlton adopting the aggressive centre-half role of England's heyday.

Gone were all those frustrating midfield passes — the tip-tapping in reverse.

England meant business and made that so obviously plain.

With only a whisker of luck those two goals could have been four and might so easily have been six.

Only a fraction of an inch, I swear, kept out a couple of flashing Peters headers.

A third from Peters, a skilfully-glanced flick, beat the 'keeper, only to be kicked off the line by Diaz.

Greaves had a cannon-ball blocked and there were two Bobby Charlton specials that Mexican defenders somehow

managed to keep out with the backs of their necks.

On top of all that was a well-taken Hunt goal which only the referee seemed to fault. He ruled him offside to the amazement of Briton and Mexican alike.

And, as the crowds streamed away from Wembley, the bookies were already chalking up England as clear favourites for the first time—at 9-2. West Germany are second favourites at 11-2 and Cup-holders Brazil have gone out to 7-1.

On this day when every England man was a hero, the captain, Bobby Moore, stood out.

Back in defence one moment, up in support of his attack the next, peppering shots against this sorely-tried Mexican wall.

'The best is ahea

● *Alf Ramsey, England's team manager, said: "I am satisfied my players gave everything they had. I am concerned about their finishing but there was never any doubt that we would win.*

"The players were over anxious before the match. The tension had been building up after the disappointing result on Monday.

"England have never been able in these two matches to settle down and play the football they are capable of.

"In our two matches our opponents have not set out to beat us, but to stop us from scoring."

● *IGNACIO TRELES, Mexican team manager said: "We came in order to obtain a draw. But when England scored we were unable to change our tactics.*

"I consider the result was just and I congratulate England team. The Char brothers were outstanding."

● *TERRY PAINE, Eng winger, revealed after match that he was concu from a blow in the face the first minute and had a bleed. He was also hurt another collision 20 min from the end.*

● *Happy Hungary — defen Kalman Meszoly and San Matrai, two heroes in the victory over Brazil — are badly hurt. Meszoly's co bone is not broken; he can m his arm freely, Matrai strai arm, has had loosen exercises.*

Jimmy Greaves has just caused the

GROUP THREE

	P	W	D	L	F	A	Pts
ortugal	2	2	0	0	6	1	4
razil	2	1	0	1	3	3	2
lungary	2	1	0	1	4	4	2
ulgaria	2	0	0	2	0	5	0

GROUP FOUR

	P	W	D	L	F	A	Pts
Russia	2	2	0	0	4	0	4
Italy	2	1	0	1	2	1	2
Chile	2	0	1	1	1	3	1
N. Korea	2	0	1	1	1	4	1

WON ONE

● Here's the Charlton thunderbolt that set England on the way to victory. Calderon is left completely helpless.

keeper to punch away but England scored because Roger Hunt pounced and shot goal No. 2 into the net.

CHARLTON

MEXICAN

ENGLAND REGAINED both their poise and their pride under the Wembley floodlights last night. Inspired by a great goal from their brilliant all-rounder, the scheming, shooting and spectacular Bobby Charlton, and lifted to new levels by two newcomers, the gifted Martin Peters and the intelligent Terry Paine, England, in beating Mexico by two goals—and it could have been six—soar to the top of Group One on goal average.

Mexico 0 England 2

by ALAN HOBY

The most important improvement in England's football lay in their new hunger for the ball and in their dramatic acceleration.

Alf Ramsey's men were far sharper and faster than against Uruguay, and with three points in their World Cup bag Ramsey must be a far happier man this morning.

Now England must continue in this free-flowing vein in their final qualifying match against France on Wednesday night.

DUAL NEED

Attack, attack, attack . . . goals, goals, goals . . . these must be the dual aims of England.

It is all very well for the smart strategists to say that we should only go for the one safe point which will see us through should it suit our purpose to finish as runners-up.

I say let us end up with a thumping victory over the capricious in-and-out Frenchmen.

To monkey around and go for a draw because we might want to avoid playing the Argentine, for example, could be an open invitation to disaster.

So my advice to England, even after this improved performance against admittedly weaker opposition, is to go all out for victory against France and also polish up their finishing—advice which applies in particular to Jimmy Greaves.

Another Englishman who caused a small flurry of concern on my part was right back George Cohen. George was scintillating in attack, but shaky in defence.

The sporting senors from Mexico played, I thought, surprisingly good football, even on defence, and were far better than I expected.

Mexico, true to prediction, fielded a deep absorbent sponge of a defence. More than 85,000 people had collected in the gigantic stadium under an overcast sky to cheer on Ramsey's men. This was the largest crowd so far in the World Cup tournament.

CHEERS FADE

But their cheers were soon muted and the chant of "England, England, England" faded when the Mexicans started with a negative 1-4-3-2 formation with the dour single-minded idea of keeping Alf Ramsey's men away from goalscoring positions.

Mexico, in what a colleague described sarcastically as "bingo football," had three stoppers in defence in addition to the traditional two full-backs.

Their line-up in this singularly unexotic Latin dish which they paraded had Jesus Del Muro operating as a sweeper up behind a four-man line of Arturo Chaires, Gustavo Pena, Gabriel Nunez, and Guillermo Hernandez. With their buzzing swarthy dynamo of an attacking left-half Isidoro Diaz linking up with

MARTIN PETERS, of England, and GABRIEL NUNEZ, of Mexico, go up for the ball—one of the tense moments in last night's World Cup battle at Wembley Stadium, London. Other World Cup pictures—Pages 14, 15.

CRACKS BARRIER

CHARLTON AND HUNT DO IT!

Salvador Reyes and Ignacio Jauregui in midfield, the Mexicans, playing in deep plum jerseys with dark blue shorts, threw back everything Bobby Moore's men could fling at them.

A tremendous flourish of cheers greeted England's first spread-eagling move when Bobby Charlton pushed the ball out to Terry Paine, who crossed to Martin Peters, playing his usual fluent professional game from midfield, whose shot flew wide.

Jimmy Greaves, sharper than I've seen him for a long time, pounced, but his shot was blocked.

Roger Hunt burst into the picture with a shot that was charged down by the Mexicans' five-man and often eight-man defence.

The boos and whistles arose from the crowd as attack after attack failed to penetrate the nimble and agile defenders from across the water.

OFF-SIDE

In the 35th minute the crowd's voice rose in a patriotic scream as Martin Peters, up on the left, crossed to Roger Hunt, who headed the ball into the net.

All around me the cheers rose, only to subside into booing as the Italian referee Concetto Lo Bello, disallowed the goal for off-side.

But England, flowing across the turf with more conviction and accuracy than at any time in this World Cup, were not to be denied and in the 37th minute Bobby Charlton suddenly sprang to his true stature.

Martin Peters, a huge success in his first World Cup game as I always thought he would be, intercepted a Mexican attack and passed to the hard working Hunt.

The Liverpool inside left pushed the ball to Charlton who set off on a wondrous old-fashioned dribble which not even Hungary's brilliant Albert could have bettered.

Jinking from side to side, from right to left, **CHARLTON** flowed across the beautiful turf for 25 yards and then let fly with a tremendous right-foot rocket.

The ball flashed diagonally from right to left and hurtled into the net past the stunned Mexican goalkeeper.

It was the loveliest sight I have seen in this World Cup.

England had scored their first Cup goal, and, suitably, the man who had done it was England's Footballer of the Year.

At last the Mexican web had been pierced. The Union Jacks waved, and Jimmy Greaves ran through again, only for his shot to be charged down by these surprisingly resolute Mexicans.

Mexico blatantly out to keep down the score, had only one really menacing attack—in the 27th minute—when Reyes hit a ball forward which bounced on Borja's dark head and ricochetted off only to be caught by the safe hands of England's goalkeeper Gordon Banks.

The Mexicans started the second half with *nine* defenders.

England, anxiously probing for a second clinching goal, nearly got it when, from Paine's corner, Peters headed diagonally down like a bayonet thrust, only for Diaz to kick off the line.

England were, as usual, playing 4-3-3, but the presence of Peters released Bobby Charlton for more penetrative duties up front.

I was not altogether happy with Nobby Stiles's contribution, despite a great deal of running about.

The England defence was vault safe as ever, with Jackie Charlton showing every promise, both in the tackle and in covering, of becoming one of the really great centre halves of this World Cup.

Ray Wilson, at left back, was his usual immaculate self, but there were one or two anxious moments on the right.

BOLD COHEN

Even so, right back George Cohen was as adventurous as usual in his overlapping raids.

The Mexicans, at last forced out of defence, began to attack in studied stylistic, but mostly predictable moves.

But one move which was not so predictable had the swaying Padilla dummying his way into the England box and forcing Banks to punch away a nasty swerving shot.

But this was an isolated sortie. Back came England, with Bobby Charlton the glittering star.

One move inspired by the astute Moore, who was "laying off" the ball with his usual skill, left Stiles free to chip the ball into the goalmouth, where Bobby Charlton, seeming to spring out of nowhere, headed the ball inches over the bar before being violently floored.

Terry Paine jinked in and beautifully beat a lunging Mexican before crossing a ball, which was cleared.

Another magnificent Charlton dribble from right to left, in which he beat the entire Mexican defence, ended when Pena, one of the three Mexican stopper half-backs, floored him just outside the penalty box

Fifteen minutes from the end England scored a superb second goal engineered by—who else? Bobby Charlton.

Deep in his own half, Charlton passed to Peters. Back to Charlton went the ball as the Manchester United all-rounder sped down the left.

A quick transfer to Jimmy Greaves and there was the little Spurs star cutting in with all his old fire and verve.

Shooting on the run, Greaves detonated Wembley as the crowd's roar rose into the very sky.

Goalkeeper Calderon, however, managed to punch out Jimmy's low drive—straight to the feet of the lurking **HUNT**, who tapped it home.

● Yes, I congratulate England. But I would add just one word of warning. They will have to raise their game still higher if they are to beat the really great teams and carry off the World Cup. . . .

ENGLAND. — Banks; Cohen, Wilson, Stiles, Charlton (J), Moore, Paine, Greaves, Charlton (R), Hunt, Peters.

MEXICO. — Calderon; Chaires, Pena, Del Muro, Jauregui, Diaz, Padilla, Nunez, Borja, Reyes, Hernandez.

Referee : C Lo Bello (Italy). **Linesmen** : M Ashkenasi (Israel), Choi Duk Ryong (N Korea).

QUOTES

Alf Ramsey (England manager) —I am satisfied my players gave everything they had. I am concerned about their finishing but there was never any doubt that we would win.

In our two matches our opponents have not set out to beat us but to stop us from scoring. Terry Paine was concussed from a blow in the face in the first minute which set his nose bleeding. He was hurt again 20 minutes from the end. Jackie Charlton was partly concussed in the first half.

Ignacio Trelles (Mexico manager)—We came in order to get a draw. We could not fight and strike well enough and quickly enough against the defence of the England team.

WORLD CUP '66: ENGLAND REACH QUARTER-FINALS WITH A 2-0 VICTORY OVER FRANCE

QUARTER-FINALS LINE-UP

No. 1	No. 2	No. 3	No. 4
ENGLAND	**URUGUAY**	**PORTUGAL**	**RUSSIA**
v	v	v	v
ARGENTINE	**W. GERMANY**	**N. KOREA**	**HUNGARY**
At Wembley	At Sheffield	At Everton	At Sunderland

All games kick off at 3 p.m. next Saturday

Winners of No. 1 quarter final play winners No. 3, at Everton, next Monday (7.30). Other semi-final at Wembley, next Tuesday (7.30)

THE AR

A left foot jab . . . a flashing header and Roger Hunt (above and below) scores twice

NOW FOR GENTINE!

France 0, England 2

ENGLAND, at last enjoying the luxury of open football, qualified for a mighty quarter-final test against Argentina at Wembley last night.

France needed to win well to survive in the Championship—but two goals by Roger Hunt killed those hopes.

England, the only side to qualify without conceding a goal, at times suggested they had at last found the right rhythm.

That they could perhaps be good enough and strong enough to crush Argentina's well-organised football at Wembley on Saturday.

By KEN JONES

But the same failings in front of goal, the same carelessness and casualness, still prevents this England side from being the power that it threatens to be.

Almost before England had begun an attack Nobby Stiles was hurt in a collision with referee Yamasaki.

Stiles recovered and England, this time confronted by a more open, more aggressive formation, established early domination.

They were building their attacks with more decision than they have previously shown in this World Cup.

A pass from deep in defence sent Jimmy Greaves away down the left wing and a curling centre had the French defence looking desperate before the ball was cleared.

Clever

A fine pass from Stiles found Roger Hunt moving intelligently through, but again the centre was cleared in the French penalty area.

A run and a shot by Greaves kept the French under pressure and Hunt was just short of reaching a shrewd Martin Peters pass that found an avenue free of defenders.

France's attacks were not designed cleverly enough to outwit England's covering, but a moment of carelessness allowed Herbin to sneak in for a header that went too close for comfort.

Interception

French centre half Budzynski had to make a great interception to prevent Bobby Charlton coming in to finish off a clever move between Ian Callaghan, Peters and Greaves, and England had by now established authority.

France's answer was to **set up the most obvious of football's defensive measures—an offside trap.**

But they executed it shrewdly and caught the England forwards far too often.

French skipper Artelesa cleared well from Greaves in the penalty area.

Then a quick French counter-attack caught England flat-footed and full-back Ray Wilson did well to clear for a corner as Gondet swept in for a shot.

Jack Charlton, emerging suddenly on to a free kick thirty yards from goal, shot fiercely and close to the French bar, and then goalkeeper Aubour was in trouble as he pushed a Callaghan cross over for a corner.

Callaghan's kick found Jack Charlton, but the centre-half's header was not powerful enough to present a real threat.

Indecision

A moment of indecision in England's penalty area brought goalkeeper Banks out to save under pressure as Bobby Moore passed back, but there was little real urgency in France's football.

A greasy pitch made tight marking and quick tackling a gamble and England were too often guilty of going too early to challenge for the ball.

The French offside trap still troubled them and Greaves had a goal ruled out by the linesman's flag.

But in the fortieth minute England got the goal for which they had worked so hard.

A fierce shot from Greaves forced Augour to concede a corner.

Greaves took it himself and when Jack Charlton's header came back off an upright, Hunt was there to score a simple goal.

The French had to come out more to strengthen their attacks and a fierce drive from full-back Bosquiet flashed wide of a post early in the second half.

Cohesion

Then for a few minutes England were switched-on—playing their passes more accurately and suggesting that at last they had complete cohesion.

But this flash of form disappeared as quickly as it had come and Stiles was booked after a challenge with full back Bosquiet.

Twelve minutes from time, England got their second, with the French still protesting over a Stiles tackle on Simon.

Callaghan crossed from the right, and Hunt, unmarked, sent home a powerful header that Aubour grasped but couldn't hold.

Taken Off

Simon then had to be taken off, following a tackle that was far too late to be offered the excuse of bad-timing.

He came back limping before the end and the French offered one last token challenge when a Hausser shot brought a brilliant save from Banks.

ENGLAND: Banks, Cohen, Wilson, Stiles, Charlton, J., Moore, Callaghan, Greaves, Charlton, R., Hunt, Peters.
FRANCE: Aubour, Djorkaeff, Artelesa (capt.), Budzynski, Bosquier, Bonnel, Herbin, Simon, Herbet, Gondet, Hausser.
REFEREE: A. Yamasaki (Peru).

A boycott on Bobby Charlton?

ENGLAND are the only team in the quarter-finals who have not conceded a goal.

Having said that, let me hastily add that they must also be the only qualifiers with three such depressing performances to their credit.

This display was the worst of all and the cheers of England's wonderful fans must have been more from relief than satisfaction at the qualifying victory.

So far it has been easy to praise an unbeaten defence, but when a team forgets the simple art of passing the ball there is no excuse at all.

England did just that to make France—like Uruguay before them—look far, far better than they have ever looked in the World Cup.

★

Skipper Bobby Moore, always seeking to do the right thing, was outstanding. Martin Peters also worked hard.

But that is more than I can say of other players.

Jimmy Greaves was always looking for goals all right, but he failed to see many of hi[s] better-placed colleagues.

For a long time I thought ther[e] must be a boycott on Bobb[y] Charlton.

Bobby was still the best di[s]tributor of the ball with h[is] limited opportunities, almo[st] repeated his Mexico goal im[]mediately before Roger Hu[nt] gave England the lead, a[nd] was the unluckiest of m[en] when he had a goal disallow[ed] for no apparent reason aft[er] 67 minutes.

Bobby also paved the way f[or] Hunt's second goal but we c[an] only hope that England ha[ve] got their worst form out [of] their systems before t[he] knock-out games arrive.

MATCH FACTS

England		France
22	GOAL ATTEMPTS	22
11	Outside penalty area	18
11	Inside penalty area	4
11	Shots saved	11
7	Shots off target	11

OFFENCES

10	Fouls	4
Nil	Handling	Nil
16	Offside	Nil
11	CORNER KICKS	9
3	Leading to goal attempts	2

NOW IT'S REALLY TOUGH, ENGLAND!

By GEORGE HARLEY

They face Argentina 'masters of defence' in quarter finals

IT'S happened . . . England, who found it difficult to penetrate the blanket defences of Uruguay and Mexico, now face Argentina, the real masters of negative football, in the quarter-final at Wembley on Saturday.

The Argentinians have been booed and barracked for their tactics in their group games at Birmingham and Sheffield. They now face a Wembley crowd ready to continue the barrage if they get the kind of football the Uruguayans have played there.

England defeated Argentina 3—1 in the last World Cup series in Chile, but lost by the only goal when the countries met in the "Little World Cup" in Brazil two years ago.

Uruguay "travel" to Sheffield for their quarter-final against West Germany, who had a taste of their negative style in the bruising battle with Argentina last Saturday.

The Iron Curtain countries are sure of one semi-finalist as Russia play Hungary in the Sunderland quarter-final. Hungary, conquerors of Brazil, will start favourites to beat the Russians, whose football has been efficient but somewhat unimaginative.

The other quarter-final is Portugal v. North Korea—England's oldest ally against a country the British Government does not recognise!

Turn over for results, reports and pictures of last night's matches

Quarter-final pairings

THE ABSENCE of Brazil and Italy from Saturday's quarter-finals (3.0) does not destroy the argument that class is the telling quality of this World Cup tournament.

For class must be defined as known and expected ability plus current form. On that basis neither of the two most illustrious absentees could claim a place.

☆

Only North Korea, allowed to slip through by the default of Italy, have reached a stage beyond their stature, and they can surely go no farther.

Their opposition, Portugal, are the most improved of the better teams in this World Cup and suffering from none of Italy's introspection, have the least troubled passage to the semi-finals.

Hungary, more imaginative than opponents Russia, have a difficult fence to scale. If enterprise triumphs, so will the Magyars, otherwise Russia's dour and methodical team march on.

Hardest quarter-final to pre-judge is West Germany v. Uruguay. Germany, like England, play in a frenzy of aggression, and could find themselves, like England, baffled by a retreating foe.

But Uruguay, in drawing two of their three games, have shown little thrust for goal. They should find it too hard to change their habits now.

In the final quarter-final England meet a similar sort of team, but on better terms. Argentina have Uruguay's discipline, Uruguay's defensive attitude, but they will be denied Uruguay's comforting thought that a draw will do.

☆

Extra time but no replays are allowed in the quarter-finals. If teams are still level after extra time the winners will be decided by drawing lots.

I believe the semi-finals will emerge as: England versus Portugal; Hungary versus West Germany.

BRIAN JAMES.

WEMBLEY
England
v.
Argentina

HILLSBOROUGH
West Germany
v.
Uruguay

GOODISON PARK
Portugal
v.
North Korea

ROKER PARK
Russia
v.
Hungary

TWO HUNT GOALS TAKE HAR

HUNT KICKS THE FIRST GOAL . . .

Purpose an

Stiles wins one tackle

By BRIAN SCOVELL

NOBBY STILES, the man England fans love to hate—and who is seen above in a mid-air duel with Budzynski—had an almost foul-free game last night.

He was penalised only twice, each time for pushing, but Peruvian referee Arturo Yamasaki spoke to him on both occasions.

If Stiles's role is to get the ball off the opposition—as Alf Ramsey is always saying—then he failed miserably. He made only seven tackles, coming out with the ball only once. And of eight attempted interceptions only four came off.

In his role of attacking midfield player, Stiles made eight long forward passes, half of which went astray. Short passes: 13 good and 5 bad. He covered a lot of ground but those figures are well below average for a half-back.

My verdict: I find it difficult to believe that he is a more useful player to England than Norman Hunter would be in the same role.

ALF RAMSEY, England manager, after the 2—0 victory over France last night: "I see no reason why we should be afraid of anybody now.

"It will be a good quarter-final against Argentina. I have reports on them and

QUOTE

quite obviously they have an excellent defence.

"This will be difficult to overcome, but I have no fears about the game.

"I am completely stunned by the amount of pressure we have been under. The players have felt that they just must not let down the supporters, their families and themselves."

● Jimmy Greaves looks a certain non-starter for the quarter final. He had two stitches put in a leg-gash last night.

)-BEAT ENGLAND TO THE TOP

. . . AND HEADS THE SECOND

GROUP ONE

England ......(1) 2 France
Hunt 2

(at Wembley)

	P.	W.	D.	L.
England	3	2	1	0
Uruguay	3	1	2	0
Mexico	3	0	2	1
France	3	0	1	2

GROUP TWC

Spain ....(1) 1 W. Germa
Fuste — Emmerich, Seeler

(at Villa Park)

	P.	W.	D.	L.
W. Germany	3	2	1	0
Argentina ...	3	2	1	0
Spain	3	1	0	2
Switzerland .	3	0	0	3

GROUP THRI

Bulgaria ......(1) 1 Hungary
Asparuhov — Davidov (, Meszoly, Bene

(at Old Trafford, Manche

	P.	W.	D.	L.
Portugal	3	3	0	0
Hungary	3	2	0	1
Brazil	3	1	0	2
Bulgaria	3	0	0	3

GROUP FOU

Chile ....(1) 1 Russia ...
Marcos — Porkujan

(at Roker Park, Sunderl

	P	W	D	L
Russia	3	3	0	0
North Korea	3	1	1	1
Italy	3	1	0	2
Chile	3	0	1	2

power

WORLD CUP '66: ENGLAND BEAT ARGENTINA TO CLAIM SEMI-FINAL PLACE

FLASHPOINT 1.—German referee Kreitlin orders off Antonio Rattin (second left). It was the incident which sparked a near-riot.

CAN THIS REALLY BE FOOTBALL?

by SAM LEITCH

A massive police escort for referee Kreitlin . . fugitive from a field of shame

AT Wembley Stadium yesterday I saw Argentine captain Antonio Rattin and his football ANIMALS disgrace the World Cup before 400 million TV viewers and 88,000 shocked spectators.

"Animals" was the word used to describe the Argentine team by England's team manager, Mr. Alf Ramsey, normally a man of few and mild words.

Was he right? Look at the picture on the left.

The little man with the bald head, the strained face and the dishevelled shirt, with the large protective policemen around him is German Rudolph Kreitlin, the referee of yesterday's quarter-final match between England and Argentina.

He wanted to keep law and order but Argentina did not want it that way. Five of their players were "booked" by Herr Kreitlin and one of these, Rattin—a Buenos Aires millionaire reputed to own three forests—was ordered off the field.

This scene is a scandalous blot on the World Cup. It is a knife in the back of football, the world's biggest game.

CAN THIS REALLY BE FOOTBALL?

While the world watched spellbound Rattin defied the referee. He would not leave the field for eight minutes. FIFA's top brass were summoned from the Royal Box to the touchline to try to get Rattin off and the game on.

Football history has been stamped on every yard of Wembley with its hectic pattern of glory and disaster. We have had rhapsodies and despair.

Yesterday we had hot-tempered, big-headed footballers from across the seas putting our national sport to shame.

The referee was punched at by track-suited Argentine team officials as the game ended. I watched the incident through my field glasses.

Forty minutes later I saw Herr Kreitlin and his Russian and Peruvian linesmen re-appear on Wembley, still with their police escort, and be smuggled out of the famous stadium via a quiet exit.

CAN THIS REALLY BE FOOTBALL?

World Cup four-page special begins on Page 17

England's winner. The scorer: Geoff Hurst, of West Ham

On Wembley's wild day...

● Wembley blow-up as Rattin (No. 10) argues with referees' chief Aston

WANTED ...a war correspondent

WEMBLEY'S near-riots yesterday brought this comment from a French sports reporter: "I won't be covering the 1970 series if this goes on. They'll be sending a war correspondent."

Other quotes last night were:

● DR. SUAREZ, the Argentinian boss: We accept defeat but feel the referee was unfair.

● ANTONIO RATTIN: When the referee sent me off I was only asking him for an interpreter. I did not insult him.

● ALBERTO GONZALES: After Rattin was sent off we played defensively hoping to last out for the toss of the coin.

● AN F.A. OFFICIAL: I have never seen anything like this in 30 years of football.

● MATT GILLIES, Leicester City's manager: If this went on in League football the crowds would stay away.

● HELMUT SCHOEN, West German team manager: I was most surprised that two Uruguayan players were sent off, but the German team has improved match by match.

● OMAR BORAS, the Uruguayan coach: Although the referee was justified in sending off the players, it would have been fair if one of the Germans had gone, too.

● ALEXANDRE BAPTISTA, Portuguese defender: The North Koreans surprised us, but even when they were three up we still thought we could win.

● A F.I.F.A. spokesman: The disciplinary committee is expected to meet on Sunday to discuss the sendings-off.

NOW FOR

But let's have no mo[re] riots, pleas[e]

England 1, Argentina 0 — By MAURIC[E]

IT WAS Wembley's blackest day — a day none of the 85,000 who saw it will ever forget.

And the 11 Englishmen now set for the first World Cup semi-final in our Soccer history will remember it most of all.

The essential fact is that England are through to a semi-final with Portugal at Wembley on Tuesday.

But, oh, what a shambles! Oh, what heavy, hard labour they made of a job that should have been easy.

Trivial foul

For German referee Rudolf Kreitlein put the skids under Argentina when he sent their strong man captain Rattin off for arguing in the 36th minute.

As he had previously booked both Rattin and Perfumo for fouls, Solari for kicking the ball away at a free-kick and Artime for what seemed to me the most trivial technical foul of all, it looked as if Herr Kreitlein was out to do more name-logging than any juvenile train-spotter.

And that the Argentinians were earmarked as victims.

Frankly, I felt sorry for these perplexed South Americans.

Some of their tackling early on may have been crude. A few tackles perhaps vicious. But they scarcely deserved this.

Yet it was England, who had opened so well, who went to pieces.

The Argentinians, almost afraid to risk a tackle for fear of adding further names to Kreitlein's catalogue, withdrew into a defensive shell.

They pulled striking forward Onega back to help in their wall of defenders, leaving themselves two men to try to pierce the England defence.

Yet England failed to crack or even fathom this improvised Argentinian blanket until 13 minutes from the end.

Then Wilson broke away on the left, passed to Peters, and the West Ham utility man found his club colleague Hurst with his cross.

Up went Hurst's head and on went England.

Hardly deservedly. And certainly not with glory.

BIG FIGHT pictures

The row goes on. Referee Kreitlein (left) orders off officials

Sent-off Rattin watches from the band's balcony

PORTUGAL

Albrecht booked

Look on it rather as a consolation goal for a lot of irritation, a lot of hard work in the first half-hour, and you won't be far wrong.

As it was, near the end the referee booked yet another Argentinian defender, Albrecht, the man sent off against West Germany.

That made five for the book, but this game was never as bad, never as fierce, never the killer that Herr Kreitlein made it appear.

He, more than anyone, in my opinion, turned potential blood-tingling drama into abject farce.

England, to be fair, had their share of fouls given against them. But none so bad as those committed early on by the Argentinians.

Certainly, no Englishman was booked. But every man in white seemed just as cowed by the referee's dramatics as the puzzled Argentinians.

The crowd's slow hand-clapping when the Argentinians were adopting virtually the only tactics left to them—time-wasting in the hope of hanging on to a draw—seemed directed as much against the clueless Englishmen as against the tip-tapping defenders.

Suppose it had been 11 against 11, what would have happened? In my opinion, England would still have won, perhaps more convincingly.

For in the first 30 minutes, for the first time in the series, they really looked like a side of World Cup final potential.

Moore and Peters were building up attacks. Ball, Hunt, and Bobby Charlton were all striking swiftly, going relentlessly forward, never giving up.

And 25-year-old Hurst, the new boy, was fitting in as though he had been used to this sort of stuff all his life.

Lost magic

England then were coming good. But after the Rattin incident and the 10-minute break while Argentinian players and officials argued with the referee, all the magic, all the fire seemed to disappear.

Perhaps they thought it would be easy. Perhaps they felt they would have extra time and extra space in which to work out their scoring moves.

Oh, what a miscalculation.

England, in the second-half, were as bad as they had previously been good.

There's an old saying in football that 10 men are often harder to beat and England certainly found it that way.

They sent cold shivers down our spines by almost allowing this two-man Argentinian attack to score a goal.

Mas, throughout the South American's most menacing forward, broke away on the left, caught Cohen one-footed and Banks too far out of goal.

A real chance, yet Mas screwed his shot a couple of inches the wrong side of a post.

No 'killer'

So what of Tuesday's match with Portugal?

Even if Jimmy Greaves is fit, and Ramsey rates him a doubtful starter, I don't think he should be picked.

On England's performance in the first 30 minutes I'd say no.

But the killer instinct—and I don't mean that in any sense of savage tackling—was certainly missing when Argentina looked lined up for the knock-out.

ENGLAND: Banks 7; Cohen 7, Charlton (J.) 7, *MOORE 8, Wilson 7; Stiles 6, Charlton (R.) 6, Peters 6; Ball 7, Hurst 7, Hunt 6.

ARGENTINA: Roma 7; Ferreiro 6, Perfumo 7, Albrecht 6, Marzolina 7; Gonzalez 7, Rattin 6, Solario 7, Onega 6; Artime 6, *MAS 8.

Referee: R. Kreitlein (Germany) 5.

HURST SC
THE SHAM

ANIMALS!
SAYS
RAMSEY

SALUTE THIS ENGLAND!
Cool heads in cauldron

ARS ABOVE LES

Quarter-finals

ENGLAND (0) 1		**ARGENTINE** (0) ...0	
Hurst			
Att.: 85,000 at Wembley			
W GERMANY (1) 4		**URUGUAY** (0) ...0	
Held, Beckenbauer, Seeler, Haller			
Att.: 40,007 at Sheffield			
PORTUGAL (2) ...5		**N. KOREA** (3) 3	
Eusebio 4 (2 pen), Augusto		Pak Seung Jin, Li Dong Woon, Yang Sung Kook	
Att.: 40,248 at Everton			
RUSSIA (1) 2		**HUNGARY** (0) ...1	
Chislenko, Porkujan		Bene	
Att.: 22,103 at Sunderland			

QUOTES

ALF RAMSEY, England manager: "It wasn't a very good game, but we won and that's the thing. Nobby Stiles was magnificent, both in his play and his conduct. I am proud he is an Englishman.

"It seems a pity that so much Argentine talent is wasted. Our best football will come against the team who come out to play football and not act as animals."

ANTONIO RATTIN, Argentina captain: "I was only trying to ask the referee for an interpreter. I did not insult him."

● England hero Geoff Hurst wheels away in triumph after scoring the goal that sank the Argentine.

WORLD CUP '66: ENGLAND ENJOY A 2-1 VICTORY OVER PORTUGAL IN SEMI-FINAL

GREAT!

ENGLAND'S GLORY BOYS

Through to the World Cup Final by 2-1

England's two-goal hero Bobby Charlton receives the final accolade as Portugal's "Black Panther" Eusebio pats his cheeks in praise at the end of a great match.

ENGLAND last night won their way to the World Cup final — for the first time in football history — by beating the Soccer giants of Portugal 2-1 at Wembley.

They proved themselves a **GREAT** team in a **GREAT** match—with a **GREAT** player in centre forward Bobby Charlton, who scored both goals.

The goals made sure that England would be in the final against West Germany at Wembley on Saturday afternoon.

The match proved more than a triumph for England. In quality, in entertainment, in sportsmanship, it restored the tarnished image of the sport.

When the final whistle went, the 90,000 crowd, biggest so far at any of the World Cup matches, went mad.

Chant

Union Jacks fluttered and a continuous chant of "England, England," went rolling across the ground. Never has an England team had such support . . . and never has one deserved it more.

Before he led his men off the field, blond England skipper Bobby Moore from West Ham shouted for three cheers for the heroic Portuguese.

The England team cheered—and so did the crowd.

Jubilant team manager Alf Ramsey said: "It was England's greatest performance since the beginning of the competition."

England start hot favourites to beat West Germany. Last night the bookmakers made them 13-8 on to win the Cup.

ENGLAND THE GREAT!

Portuguese goalkeeper Jose Pereira goes down on his knees to clasp a shot from Roger Hunt (white shirt) in the World Cup semi-final at Wembley

Bobby Charlton scores England's second goal from a Hurst pass.

Gordon Banks is beaten for the first time—by Eusebio's penalty kick.

WELL DONE, RAMSEY

By JOHN MORGAN
The Sports Editor

ALF RAMSEY—you know the name. He is the man who was a meticulous defender for Tottenham and England.

He is the man who went to Ipswich as manager and by sheer calculated planning raised what was a Soccer Cinderella team team through to the championships of every Division—including the First—in the Football League.

He is the man who took over from Walter Winterbottom as manager of the England team three and a half years ago and has suffered as much criticism as any I know in sport.

He baffled the critics—newspapers not least of all—by his experiments with players.

He was roundly lashed for shunning conventions and daring to play England teams without such things as recognised wingers.

It was not so long ago that a lot of people were asking: "Is Ramsey the right man for England?"

SUPERB

Through it all — the criticism and the setbacks—Alf Ramsey made only two observations.

His first: "Judge me in retrospect AFTER the World Cup."

His second: "England will win it."

Well, they have not yet won it. But last night—by that superb display from an England team that was so proud to be wearing the shirts of their country—Ramsey was publicly vindicated.

England answered all her critics.

Today there will be resounding applause for the man who inspired it.

The Alf Ramsey I know will not yet accept that his mission is accomplished. There will be no counting of chickens until the final whistle in Saturday's Final.

But for me—and thousands more—he has done a brilliant job for Soccer, and for England.

TWO-GOAL BOBBY PUTS ENGLAND IN FINAL—THEN JACK SLIPS UP

By KEN JONES

ENGLAND rose from a great match, on a night of almost unbearable tension, to take a proud place in the World Cup Final last night.

They went there with every Wembley watcher battling with the suffocation of excitement, as the skilled and courageous Portuguese mounted their last wave of attacks.

Semi-Final	
ENGLAND	**2**
R. Charlton 31 min., 80 min.	
PORTUGAL	**1**
Eusebio, pen., 84 min.	
HT: 1—0.	**Att.: 90,000.**

Stamina draining from their legs, realising suddenly that triumph could still be snatched from their grasp, England in the end had to survive six minutes that I for one could not bear to watch again.

Six minutes when a one goal lead threatened to evaporate.

And in the end it was the professionalism of their finest professional that saw them through.

Nobby Stiles, with awareness that was amazing even in him, suddenly sensed and saw a hole being torn in the sagging curtain of his defence.

Plunge

Like a hawk, he plunged at the point of impending disaster, smothering a Simoes shot that was already being directed at the back of England's net.

Simoes rolled over, hurt, frustrated, foiled by a little man who rose out of his success, waving angry arms at the England men who were to blame.

But not even that was enough to puncture the tension. England were still not safe.

From an attack on the right, the cool Coluna mustered all his skill and cunning into a shot that began to bend and seemed to bend again as Gordon Banks, twirling backwards, answered the call, and put the ball away for a corner.

Finest

Then England were suddenly safe, suddenly through, to face West Germany at Wembley on Saturday.

What went before was the supreme answer to those who have found nothing in this World Cup, who have found only something to criticise.

As a match, it was the finest Wembley has witnessed since West Ham went there to win in the European final against Munich two years ago.

At last there was a game that lived up to the true traditions of World Cup football. A game that could take a proud place in the competition's history.

The anger and incident that has played too big a part in the past two weeks disappeared.

Two teams staged football of great quality and sportsmanship that has rarely been equalled in a contest of such importance.

A shrewd England decision made before the match did not send one man in search of Eusebio, one man to snuff out his skill and to put him out of the match.

Instead, Eusebio was taken by the man nearest to him.

And this made him a far different footballer from the one who heads the list of World Cup goal-scorers.

I have always suspected that his inability to play with others, his complete individualism, leaves him short of true world class.

This great striker of a ball was rarely more than an ordinary player last night.

Classic

Certainly, he struck shots with fierce intent twice close to the posts that Banks guarded with such skill.

But it was England who produced the goals that lifted this game into a classical contest between two fine sides.

After squandering opportunity in the manner they have so often done before, England struck in the thirty-first minute against a Portuguese defence that always suggested it would offer a chance.

A through ball from full back Ray Wilson sent Roger Hunt hurrying through, and brought goalkeeper Pereira from his line to meet him.

The ball broke out invitingly to the feet of Bobby Charlton. He side-footed it home with calm authority, through the wreckage of Portugal's defence.

Their goal sparked England into confident, fluent football — but they were stopped, first by a desperate Portuguese defence, and then by Portugal's flair for imaginative attack.

It was the swift Simoes and the tall Torres who now appeared as the masters—and England's covering became careless.

In the second half England threatened to lose everything, losing their grip on the match, losing the ball too often in the tackle, and rarely getting it back.

But gradually England got back into the game with Hurst and Hunt creating wider avenues up front, and with little Alan Ball battling to show others that the ball could be won, and kept.

Superb

Then in the eightieth minute England scored a superb goal.

It began with a shrewd, headed clearance by Jack Charlton. It went from Wilson to Ball. From Ball to Moore, and across field to George Cohen.

From there it went forward, and Hurst was on it, boring his way through, holding up a challenge, and placing the ball in the path of Bobby Charlton.

Charlton seemed to settle in his stride, and then hit it with stunning force past Pereira.

It looked all over, but from a cross on the right, danger suddenly appeared.

Banks, seemingly bustled by Torres, lost out in the challenge, and Jack Charlton had to handle the header away.

Eusebio took the spot kick, stroking it calmly home, and the battle was on.

In the end England were through, receiving the acclaim of their fans, and with the Portuguese consoling a tearful Eusebio down the tunnel.

TEAMS

ENGLAND.—Banks, Cohen, Charlton J., Moore, Wilson, Stiles, Charlton R., Ball, Hurst, Hunt, Peters.

PORTUGAL. — Pereira, Festa, Baptista, Carlos, Hilario, Graca, Coluna, Augusto, Eusebio, Torres, Simoes.

Referee: P. Schwinte (France).
Linesmen: K. Zecevic (Yugoslavia), A. Yamasaki (Peru).

MATCH FACTS

England		Portugal
19	GOAL ATTEMPTS	32
11	Outside pen. area	23
8	Inside pen. area	9
13	Shots saved	18
4	Shots off target	13
14	OFFENCES	4
8	Fouls	4
2	Handling	Nil
4	Offside	Nil
7	CORNER KICKS	13
1	Lead'g to goal atts.	5
51	Times ball put out of play	33

● *EUSEBIO, in tears, is comforted by a team official as he leaves the Wembley pitch, his dream of a World Cup Final wrecked.*

Ramsey plan cages the Black Panther

By BRIAN SCOVELL

EUSEBIO (the Portuguese say it Yew-say-bew) failed to live up to his billing as the world's No. 1 footballer. Or rather, he wasn't allowed to.

Alf Ramsey had him cunningly played out of the game by keeping Nobby Stiles deep, and letting the nearest man to Eusebio stand off in front of him.

Rarely did anyone tackle him. It was like watching a black panther in a cage, pawing in frustration but unable to break out.

The great man put in eight goal attempts, the most dangerous being a volley in the 35th minute that was brilliantly saved by Banks. Eusebio scored his eighth goal of the tournament, but it was a straightforward penalty.

Banks, obviously forgetting which side Eusebio put his two penalties against Korea, went the wrong way.

In the first half we all wondered when the wandering Eusebio was going to cut loose. The answer soon came. He wasn't going to.

Well up

His work rate—19 accurate short passes, four inaccurate; and two good long passes, one bad one — fell off to such an extent that he made only nine passes in the second half—though admittedly he played well up in the second half.

Eusebio was fouled only once—by Peters. No one came close enough after that.

He made seven dribbles in the game, but at the end of them it was the same story, nowhere to go, no one to pass to.

If Eusebio failed last night does this mean that two-goal Bobby Charlton succeeds him as man of the tournament and the new king of world football?

I don't think so . . . unless Charlton wins the final on Saturday on his own.

Eusebio, on his earlier form which he could not reproduce last night, must keep the title. Last night it was a win for the system.

This was England's greatest performance since the beginning of the competition

THAT was England manager Alf Ramsey's summing-up of last night's match. He went on: "Portugal were a very capable and good side. It was a pity that one team had to be beaten.

"We have a very good side, very efficient, and they have done all that has been asked of them. In the second half we lost a little of our composure. This was understandable following the punishing match on Saturday, when some of the players were in distress in the second half against Argentina because of the heat."

THE FINAL? "I do not think West Germany will provide a bigger challenge than Portugal."

GREAVES'S INJURY? "It should heal in the next few days."

UNFORTUNATE CHOICE

ALF RAMSEY made a reference to his "animals" remarks which earned him reproof by the FIFA disciplinary committee. He said: "I think the less said the better. I was unfortunate in my choice of words. I am placed in the position of answering questions under such conditions because of my job. It does not excuse my choice of words."

OTTO GLORIA, Portugal's coach, said: "My players thought they should have had a penalty in the second half, but the referee is the supreme judge.

"England play as football ought to be played. Germany rely on force."

ENGLAND have equalled the all-time World Cup defensive record by conceding only one goal in reaching the Final. Only two other countries have done this—Uruguay when they won the first tournament in 1930, and Hungary when runners-up in 1938.

UNBEATEN RUN

ENGLAND'S present run is 15 matches unbeaten (13 wins, 2 draws, goals 31-7). Their last 12 games have produced 11 wins and a draw (goals 26-5).

BOBBY CHARLTON, with two goals last night, has scored three in the tournament, equalling England's highest individual total of World Cup goals—three by Nat Lofthouse (1954) and Roger Hunt (this year).

WORLD CUP '66: ENGLAND WIN WORLD CUP FINAL WITH A 4-2 DEFEAT OF WEST GERMANY

ENGLAND, LOVELY ENGLAND!

WITH the very last kick of the match, after 120 grueling minutes, Geoff Hurst scored a magnificent goal to give England a 4—2 victory over West Germany, after extra time, in the World Cup final at Wembley yesterday.

● Moore chaired by Hurst and Wilson.

ENGLAND

Banks
Leicester

Cohen Fulham — **Charlton, J.** Leeds — **Moore** West Ham — **Wilson** Everton

Stiles Manchester Un. — **Charlton, R.** Manchester Un. — **Peters** West Ham

Ball Blackpool — **Hunt** Liverpool — **Hurst** West Ham

●

Emmerich — **Seeler** — **Held**

Overath — **Haller** — **Beckenbauer**

Schnellinger — **Weber** — **Schulz** — **Höttges**

Tilkowski

WEST GERMANY

Referee: G. Dienst (Switzerland).
Linesmen: K. Galba (Czechoslovakia), T. Bakhramov (USSR).

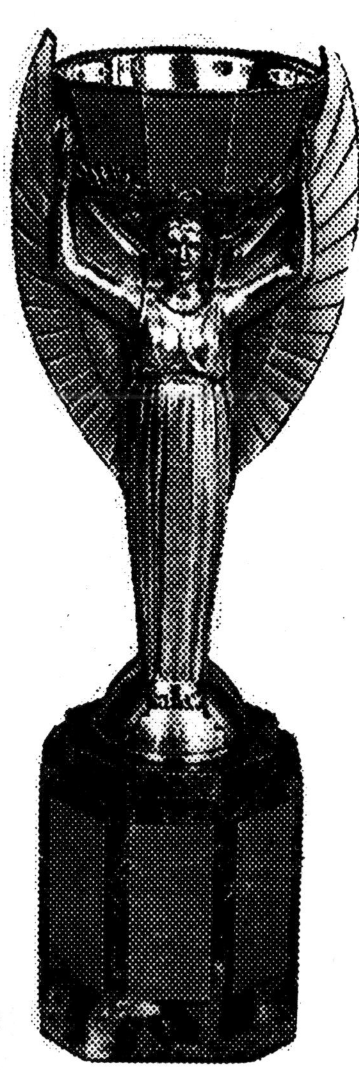

That slim gold cup is ours

0-1: Haller for Germany—10 minutes

1-1: Hurst for England—16 minutes

2-1: Peters for England—75 minutes

2-2: Weber for Germany—89 minutes

3-2: Hurst, again, for England—100 minutes

4-2: And Hurst, once more, with the last kick

A TEAM OF 11 HEROES

WEMBLEY has never seen its like. This was the day manager Alf Ramsey earned the reward of three patient, often plodding years of patient preparation.

Not only Ramsey, but every member of his team on an afternoon, grim and overcast, when the sun broke through to highlight splendidly the victory scene.

As they paraded with the Jules Rimet trophy, this vast stadium, scene of so many memorable clashes, roared out the new National Anthem, "When the Saints Go Marching In," while the band belted it out.

This was something that will always live in our memories, those of us privileged to be there for England's greatest Soccer triumph.

COMMENT by KEN HAWKES

Even the Merseysiders, bearing aloft the banner "After Liverpool, England are the greatest," must have questioned its wording in those emotion-charged moments.

How does one pick out England men for special praise? Better, surely, to say it was a team effort, and leave it at that. But there must be a special accolade for skipper Bobby Moore, whose inspiration has been such a determining factor during the past few weeks, and much longer than that.

Those great-hearted little men, Nobby Stiles and Alan Ball, also typified the never-say-die fighting spirit that has carried England to glory the cynics said could never be.

And as a Londoner, I must find place for the other pair of West Ham's trio of heroes—Geoff Hurst and the intelligent Martin Peters, who got the second goal. Hurst, scorer of the first treble in any World Cup Final, gave England a comfortable winning margin, after long, dragging minutes of extra-time suspense, with his last kick.

Goalkeeper extraordinary Gordon Banks, the solidly dependable Ray Wilson and George Cohen, the dominant figures of Jack Charlton and his brother, Bobby, the far-ranging Roger Hunt . . . heroes, every one of them.

And that's the complete line-up, isn't it? Well, this was, above all, a team effort, wasn't it? Let's leave any minor failings for the inquest-lovers. This was England's day!

ENGLAND—CHAMPIONS OF THE WORLD

AROUND 5.15 p.m. YESTERDAY the most triumphant and tumultuous din I have ever heard rose from the stands and terraces of Wembley Stadium. From every side of what has been described as "this historic cathedral of football" a blaze of Union Jacks waved as people, unashamedly gripped by emotion and patriotism, danced, wept, and hugged each other.

For as the whistle of Swiss referee Gottfried Dienst sounded the end of this truly manly and magnificent battle it meant that at last West Germany had conceded defeat.

England had WON. . . . England who gave Soccer to the rest of the earth were FOOTBALL CHAMPIONS OF THE WORLD.

Never in its long history of sporting spectaculars had Wembley witnessed such scenes or such action on this glorious stretch of turf.

For this was the match to end all matches.

TITANIC

This was a titanic struggle, which had everything, played for long stretches against a Wagnerian backdrop of dark clouds.

For two hours the 93,000 spectators who had paid a record-breaking £300,000, plus the invisible audience of 400 million television viewers throughout the world, had stood on a tightrope of drama and almost unbearable excitement.

They had seen three dynamic goals by West Ham's GEOFFREY HURST.

They had seen Alan Ball, that little, much-criticised, red-haired bundle of dynamite, emerge as man of the match.

They had seen Bobby Moore never more majestic and assured in a defence which, understandably in the frying tension, had wilted at odd moments in the most alarming manner.

But, above all, what they will tell their grandchildren in the years to come is that it was English nerve and English heart which finally overcame the tenacious resistance of Uwe Seeler and his white-shirted men.

They will in particular relate that their hearts thudded and raced as, with England leading 2—1, Germany equalised 15 seconds from the end of ordinary time.

With only these fractions of moments separating England from winning the World Cup, referee Dienst awarded what I thought was an unfair free kick against England's noble centre half Jackie Charlton when he climbed up to head the ball away.

The Swiss referee penalised Charlton for going up over the back of Germany's No. 1 star, Siegfried Held, which in Germany means "hero."

But I was convinced that Held, a rangy, fluid, fast-dribbling forward, had "made a back" for Charlton.

However, in the resultant blur of action Emmerich drove a blasting free kick towards the English goal.

AGONISING

The ball vanished into a mêlée of white and red shirts—England were playing in red—and there was the blond Helmut Haller guiding the ball with his hand to the right where, after agonising moments, West Germany's stern WOLFGANG WEBER lashed it into goal.

This was a ghastly moment for England with the World Cup apparently in their grasp.

As the referee's whistle shrilled the end of 90 minutes players collapsed on the grass.

For the pace had been electric and the football superb.

Ray Wilson had to receive attention on the touchline for cramp, and several of the German players were rubbing their legs with the mounting exhaustion which this headlong duel had produced in the players.

Now we were into extra time and the tension was almost unendurable.

With legs weighted down like lead and breath rasping in the lungs, the tempo had inevitably dropped.

Schnellinger, Germany's polished left-back from Milan, who had set out to mark Alan Ball but in the end had found himself outspeeded and outsmarted, came to a halt with cramp.

Goalkeeper Hans Tilkowski was limping badly as Bobby Charlton's waspish shot from brother Jackie's downward header thrashed inches outside the post.

Then, with Ball leading the charge of the red shirts, flicking and darting into every available open space like a scarlet firefly, England scored the golden goal which set them on the last short haul to the tip of this football Everest.

SWOOPED

With 10 minutes of the extra time showing on our stopwatches, Ball swooped on the ball and swung it over. Amid a hullabaloo of sound, HURST, that indomitable and heroic figure, twisted on to it and crashed it with his right foot against the underside of the bar.

There was an awful moment of eternity as the ball ricocheted down, and from where I sat appeared to hit the turf just inside the white line.

But many foreign observers sitting in a line with the German goal thought that the ball had not crossed the line. So did the entire German team.

As the goal roar resounded through the stadium the Germans ran to the Russian linesman, Tofik Bakhramov.

There was another paralysing passage of seconds while the white-haired Russian nodded his head vigorously as referee Dienst interrogated him in a short but decisive dialogue which confirmed that England had scored.

A controversial goal maybe . . . a goal which had its doubters true . . . But fair compensation, I thought, for the decision 15 seconds from time which had earlier robbed England of victory.

In any case England, who created more chances than West Germany, clinched this marvellous match when, in the very last seconds Hurst, pounding on to a long ball, dredged the last shreds of energy from his aching legs, shrugged off the challenge of a desperate German defender, and lashed the ball triumphantly and heroically into the net. (4—2)

ERUPTED

England were home, and in the next few seconds the whole arena erupted in joy and gratitude.

Below me, as the England team ran off, manager Alf Ramsey at last stepped forward into the spotlight he so detests to congratulate each of his Englishmen—the team he has always believed in despite the critics.

Ramsey, who refused to let his team chair him, had a particularly warm hug for Bobby Moore and Alan Ball.

I admit I have been one of Ball's critics. But I can say with sincere delight that I was wrong and that 21-year-old Ball was the tiny tornado who rallied England when West Germany, through the clever midfield build-up of Haller, Overath, and Seeler, looked like taking charge.

Another titanic wave of cheering eddied all round us as Bobby Moore led his team on a victory lap with the golden Jules Rimet trophy held aloft.

The England players were still trying to involve the manager who had told them over and over that they would win the World Cup but Alf Ramsey refused to share their moment of splendour. Typically he held back.

I take nothing away from some magnificent West German football when I say that England in the end were worthy victors, although the game of football itself was the greatest victor of all.

It was a heartbreaking moment for left back Ray Wilson when he made his first mistake of the entire World Cup series in the 12th minute.

TENACIOUS

Held, that tenacious German, out on his favourite left side of the field, had crossed from a corner when Wilson, amid a collective gulp of horror, headed straight to HALLER on the right.

The quick-thinking German forward shot and the ball seemed to skid past Jackie Charlton into the net and past the best goalkeeper in the 1966 World Cup, Gordon Banks, who was probably unsighted.

This was a body blow, and the black, orange, and yellow banners of West Germany were brandished from side to side of the stadium.

But five minutes later Germany's Wolfgang Overath fouled Moore, and while the referee was still lecturing the German, the English captain pinpointed the most elegant of free kicks into the heart of the German defence.

Distracted for a moment, not one of the German "wall," not even the relentless sweeper Willi Schulz or their strong tackling Horst Hottges, spotted Hurst starting his run from the angle of the box.

It was a brilliant piece of intuitive thinking — first-class anticipation. For before a single German could explode into action HURST completed his great run with a soaring header which billowed the back of the net with goalkeeper Tilkowski utterly helpless (1—1).

If I had to single out the first three Englishmen from this dedicated and unyielding World Cup squad of ours I would have to name Hurst, Moore, and Ball, with the scintillating Blackpool star just edging the other two out as our World Cup hero No. 1.

The tactical pattern of play flowed and eddied, but the disappointments as the struggle progressed were Bobby Charlton, who looked tired, and West Germany's stylish attacking wing half Franz Beckenbauer.

Even so, as the thunderclouds gathered, the England defence suffered its most indecisive period of the tournament.

Our team seemed to run down both in energy and enterprise.

GREAT SAVES

Indeed, in the 36th minute a whole army of butterflies must have swirled in the stomachs of every Englishman as Gordon Banks made an absolutely out-of-this-world save from a scorching Overath drive from inside the box.

Banks got his hands to the ball but could not hold it. Yet this great goalkeeper, sliding on to his rump, saved again, close in, from another piledriver by Lothar Emmerich.

In the 42nd minute Banks had to leap like a trapeze artist to fingertip over a swerving, diabolical, 40-yard brute of a shot from Uwe Seeler. And so it went on, a game which, as time ate up the second half, resembled a blend of the endurance of an Olympic marathon, the sudden thrills of a film epic, and all the starlit drama of great theatre.

But towards the end of the second period England got their second wind and, fittingly, it was Ball, dribbling in from the right, who forced Tilkowski to touch the ball round the post for the corner which was indirectly to produce England's second goal.

But by this time nerves were raw from suspense, and one wondered how much more we could take when from the corner there was a wild skirmish of shirts. Hurst shot and a German defender mis-cued his clearance right into his own box, where MARTIN PETERS—yes another West Ham man!—who has played such an important part in England's midfield set-up, cracked the ball into the net to put England 2—1 up.

The rest is history.

But when the verdict of the great world jury on the 1966 World Cup is rendered there can be little doubt that England's "wingless wonders," playing vintage 20th-century football in the 4-3-3 style laid down by their manager, were the better team.

All I can add, amid the cooler moments which followed the frenzy of feeling which heralded the end of quite the most extra-ordinary game I have ever seen, is that every Englishman—and German too—gave his "all" in a 120-minute outpouring of talent and entertainment.

No more can be asked. And no one who saw this historic World Cup Final can deny England their "finest hour."

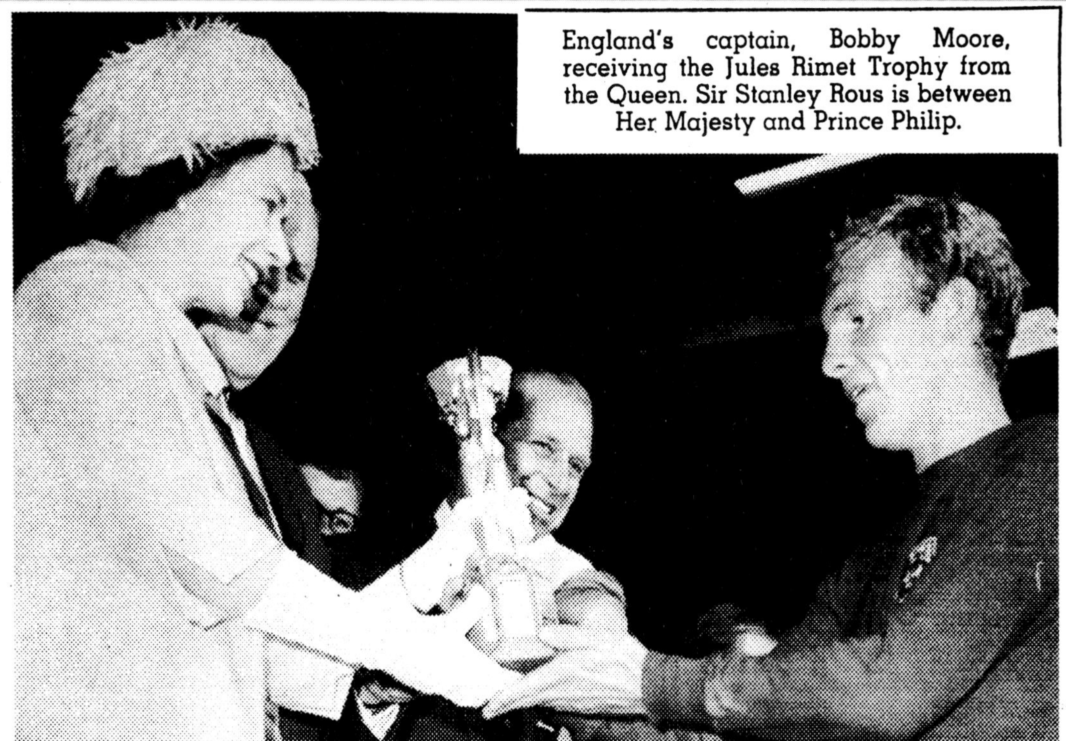

England's captain, Bobby Moore, receiving the Jules Rimet Trophy from the Queen. Sir Stanley Rous is between Her Majesty and Prince Philip.

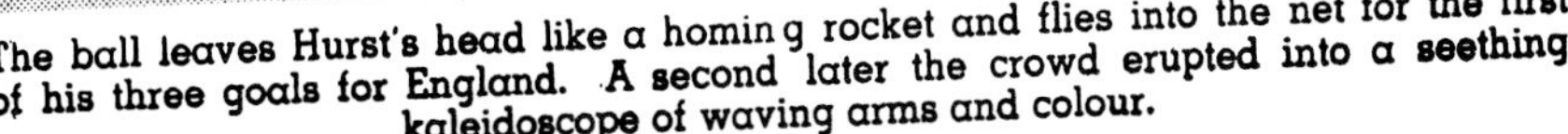

The ball leaves Hurst's head like a homing rocket and flies into the net for the first of his three goals for England. A second later the crowd erupted into a seething kaleidoscope of waving arms and colour.

GORDON BA

HURST HAT-TRICK CLINCHES IT FOR ENGLAND

England 4, West Germany 2
Hurst 3, Peters — Haller, Weber
(after extra time) — Att. 93,000

MATCH FACTS

ENGLAND
GOAL ATTEMPTS: 45 (4 goals, 1 hit post, 10 saved, 6 blocked, 3 deflected, 21 wide or high).
CORNERS: 6.
FOULS: 22 (including 3 "hands").
THROW-INS: 36.
OFFSIDE: 4.
GOAL KICKS: 16.

WEST GERMANY
GOAL ATTEMPTS: 37 (2 goals, 9 saved, 9 blocked, 5 deflected, 12 wide or high).
CORNERS: 12.
FOULS: 16 (including 3 "hands").
THROW-INS: 19.
OFFSIDE: 4.
GOAL KICKS: 24.

HOW ENGLAND GOT THERE

(Group games) drew Uruguay 0—0, beat Mexico 2—0, beat France 2—0.

Quarter-final: beat Argentine 1—0.

Semi-final: beat Portugal 2—1.

A DREAM BECOMES REALITY FOR ARCHITECT OF ENGLAND'S TRIUMPH

PROUD MOMENT for the England team manager, Alf Ramsey, as he kissed the Jules Rimet Trophy held by captain Bobby Moore.

ORGE COHEN

JACK CHARLTON

BOBBY MOORE

RAY WILSON

NOBBY STILES

BBY CHARLTON

MARTIN PETERS

ALAN BALL

ROGER HUNT

GEOFF HURST

BOBBY CHARLTON SCORES A RECORD-BREAKING 45TH GOAL FOR ENGLAND

BOBBY'S RECORD BUSTER

Superb goal puts England back in the old groove

By KEN JONES

BOBBY CHARLTON broke England's scoring record and the hearts of a persistent Swedish side with a goal of stunning brilliance at Wembley last night.

Records are meant to be broken this way—with power and grace, in one of the finest of sporting settings and with a vast audience applauding. Charlton began his run forty yards from goal in the thirty-eighth minute and sped into the space that opened before him.

He swayed clear of a despairing challenge and hit a shot of breath-taking power past the helpless Swedish goal-keeper Sven Larsson.

Then he spun away, answering the salute of a 72,000 crowd and turning to receive the praise of his teammates.

ENGLAND - - -		**3**
Peters, Charlton, Hunt		
SWEDEN - - - -		**1**
Andersson		
H-T: 2—0. Att.: 72,500.		

SWEDISH 'KEEPER IN HOSPITAL

SWEDEN goalkeeper Sven Larsson was detained at St. George's Hospital, Hyde Park Corner, last night for treatment on a neck injury.

Team manager Orvar Bergmark said: "We do not know what the full trouble is but he has concussion and does not know where he is."

CHARLTON HITS GREAT RECORD-BREAKING GOAL

PETER LORENZO reports from Wembley: England 3, Sweden 1

BOBBY CHARLTON became England's record marksman at Wembley last night.

It was a goal that even by Charlton's illustrious standards will rank as one of the most spectacular and dynamic of his magnificent career.

It came in the 39th minute and dwarfed everything that preceded and followed it.

Charlton, the only survivor of the 22 who were at Wembley nine years ago when Sweden beat England 3-2, ran on to a short pass from Colin Bell 10 yards inside the Swedish half.

Charlton drifted past one blue-shirted defender, jinked past another, feinted to shoot with his left foot, then pulled the ball on to his right to glide effortlessly past another helpless Swedish "statue" before crashing a superb shot into the top corner from 22 yards.

DELIGHTED

The 72,500 crowd and a swarm of delighted England colleagues greeted this gem of a goal. It was the 45th of Charlton's distinguished career, one more than Jimmy Greaves, who had held the record for so long.

I saw Charlton score with a thundering volley in his first England game—against Scotland at Hampden Park 10 years ago.

This one matched it for brilliance and spectacle—what a perfect way to set a record.

Charlton never came out for the second half. He was replaced by Geoff Hurst.

Though Bobby was said to have an abrasion on his left shin and had been taken off as a precaution, it nevertheless provided a perfect opportunity to give Hurst, a long-time sufferer with back trouble, a vigorous test to prove his fitness to travel to Italy for the last stages of the European Nations' Cup next month.

SPECTACULAR

A minute before the Charlton spectacular Martin Peters, who has been England's most consistent scorer these last five games and has failed to score in only one of them, headed England into the lead with a characteristic close-range header.

Again Charlton had a talented foot in this goal.

Roger Hunt and Charlton, noting the slackness of the Swedish cover, ran quickly for a short corner on the right. Hunt tapped the ball to Charlton and Bobby neatly returned it and Peters darted to the near post to head in Hunt's cross.

This was a leisurely but still slick triumph by England, exacting full revenge for that 1959 defeat, when Sweden became only the second foreign nation to defeat England on her own soil.

Hungary were the first and Austria the last, three years ago.

England were in effortless command in the second-half and went three up after 70 minutes.

After a tenacious run by right-back Newton, left-back Knowles crashed a storming shot against the bar. Hurst went up to challenge for the rebound and the ball dropped invitingly back for Hunt to crack it home.

It was an excellent debut for the two newcomers, goalkeeper Alex Stepney and front-runner Bell.

Stepney has not been in the most inspiring form for Manchester United lately, but he never made a mistake last night.

SEVERAL CHANCES

Because of the adventurous nature of the game, he had several chances to show his merit, and none better than a minute after the Charlton goal when he showed great skill and timing to race out of his goal to deflect a shot from centre-forward Ejderstedt, who was through on his own.

Before and after Stepney showed the form that will encourage Sir Alf Ramsey, should he have to pitch Stepney into the Nations Cup matches.

Bell, wearing the No. 7 shirt, toiled as hard, and at times as skilfully as Alan Ball, the normal occupant.

Bell fitted well and intelligenty into the midfield section, and was willing, when the situation was right, to have a go himself.

The four World Cup-winners on duty, Bobby Moore, Peters, Hunt—and Bobby Charlton in the first half—gave the team a solid basis. Even though the personnel were so changed there was still an unmistakable similarity between the football of this and the side that won the World Cup two years ago.

The only unhappy incident came five minutes from time when Swedish goalkeeper Larsson was carried off after a mid-air clash with Mullery.

The sight of the anxious Swedish players desperately calling for a stretcher suggested the Swede had been seriously hurt.

SPECULATION

It was fortunately only concussion. Nils Hult replaced him in goal.

Mullery was unhurt. He had again played so ably and there must now be considerable speculation whether a fully fit Nobby Stiles would take over from him.

In the final minute Sweden's substitute centre-forward Andersson scored his side's consolation goal after drifting by Hunter in the penalty box.

There was just time to place the ball on the centre spot before Swiss referee Ottma Huber blew the final whistle on a most competent, relatively leisurely England conquest.

ENGLAND: **Stepney** (Man. United), **Newton** (Blackburn), **Knowles** (Spurs), **Mullery** (Spurs), **Labone** (Everton), **Moore** (captain), **Peters** (West Ham), **Bell** (Man. City), **Charlton** (Man. United), **Hunt** (Liverpool), **Hunter** (Leeds). Sub.: **Hurst** (West Ham).

SWEDEN: Sven-Gunnar Larsson, Carlsson, Kristensson, Nordqvist, Grip, Eriksson, Bo Larsson, Nordahl, Ejderstedt, Lindman, Persson. Sub.: **Andersson.**
Referee: **O. Huber (Switzerland).**

And that's No. 45. Bobby Charlton's shot hurtles past Sweden's goalkeeper at Wembley last night to set an England scoring record. *Picture: MONTE FRESCO.*

Martin Peters (England) beats Krister Kristensson (Sweden) and heads in England's first goal

Bobby Charlton excels in competent victory

By ALBERT BARHAM: England 3, Sweden 1

England expects so much of England these days that even a 3-1 victory over Sweden last night was not considered sufficient judging by the whistles of the 72,500 at Wembley. But what was the match really all about? It was primarily a build-up for the European Championships early next month and the opportunity was gladly taken by Sir Alf Ramsey, England's team manager, to introduce a number of the less prominent members of England's squad.

In my opinion this was a good, workmanlike performance by England, impressive at times and interesting too. The manner in which the victory was obtained was just as important as—or more so than—the result, with the broader picture of the European Championships in mind. Nobody could say that any of the newly-introduced players or those who had been brought back into the team were below the now high standard of methodical play which has brought admiration and envy from so many foreign observers and officials.

Depth of talent

Above all, perhaps, there was shown again, to the envy of the Continental countries, the depth of England's talent. The introduction of fresh blood in no way impairs the impressive performance of the side as a whole.

It might be argued that so much has been promised so often by England but so little fulfilled; in the last 22 matches England have played at Wembley only once—against Wales 18 months ago when they won 5-1—has there been more than a two-goal margin. Sweden were the second side, in 1959, to beat England on their own soil and indeed they had until last night never lost here. So that little matter was avenged.

It was, of course, on the cards that England would win handsomely. One must not forget that Sweden have lost 50 of their best players to other nations in the past few years. They had also drawn with and lost to Spain, whom England had twice beaten. But one must emphasise again that it was the authoritative manner in which England won which was of prime consideration.

One moment above all stood out in this match for individual brilliance. It belonged to Bobby Charlton, who scored a goal which will go down as one of his finest. It was scored as we have seen so many of his great goals scored, with a move inside the defender—this time the unfortunate Nordquist—and a thunderous shot into the roof of the net. It gave him not only the satisfaction of a fine achievement but it also now makes him England's leading scorer, with 45 goals, one more than Jimmy Greaves.

The match was marred by an accident to Sven Larsson, Sweden's goalkeeper. Larsson came to Stoke a couple of years ago, but his registration was not accepted. Last night, returning to England for the first time since then, he collided heavily with Mullery six minutes from the end of the match and was carried off on a stretcher to have his head X-rayed.

Consolation goal

Hult replaced him; and it was another substitute—this time Anderson, who came on at half time for Ejderstedt—who scored Sweden's consolation goal in the second minute of injury time. England also made a substitution at half time, for Charlton, after his magnificent goal in the thirty-eighth minute, had an abrasion on his left shin, and was replaced by Hurst of West Ham when the game restarted.

Stepney, protected by the great umbrella of England's defence, played in his first international most impressively. So too, did Bell and this great strength in midfield, where Mullery looked the most improved international player, held the key to England's victory. Once again, however, it was the generalship of Moore which was as much as anything responsible for Sweden's discomfiture in attack. They were not really strong enough yet, as their manager promised, they put on a good display for the millions watching back home in Scandinavia.

More industrious

England were faster to the ball, quicker to the tackle and more industrious. Yet in the first half Sweden might well have had a couple of goals. Instead there was once again the moral that it really is no use making chances if they are not turned into goals. Their chances came in a horrid moment for England when Moore, obviously impeded by Eriksson, was left with the best advantage he could get. Stepney, however, raced out, reached out an arm and pulled down the ball. It went to Ejderstedt.

There he was with a defence momentarily disorganised and a goalkeeper out of position, but he ballooned the chance over the bar. The Swedes came again, this time in a swarm with Lindman, Erikkson and Ejderstedt moving into a delightful bout of passing. Once again Ejderstedt wasted a chance, prodding the ball wide.

ENGLAND.—Stepney (Man. Utd.); Newton (Blackburn R.), Knowles (Spurs); Mullery (Spurs), Labone (Everton), Moore (West Ham Utd.); Peters (West Ham Utd.), Bell (Man. City), Charlton (Man. Utd.), Hunt Liverpool), Hunter (Leeds Utd.).

SWEDEN.—Larsson S-G; Karlsson, Kristensson; Nordquist, Grip, B. Larsson; Lindman, Eriksson, Ejderstedt, Nordahl, Persson.

Referee: O. Huber (Switzerland).

GOAL ACE CHARLTON

MANCHESTER UNITED BECOME FIRST ENGLISH TEAM TO WIN EUROPEAN CHAMPIONS' CUP

EXTRA-TIME CHAMPS

Bobby Charlton does a vertical take-off to show his feelings after heading Manchester United's first goal seven minutes after the interval. Then he hammered the fourth.

Charlton, Best and Kidd blast United to Cup

By KEN JONES

MANCHESTER UNITED realised their greatest dream when they won the European Cup at Wembley last night after eleven years of endeavour.

Three goals in the first ten minutes of extra time by George Best, birthday boy Brian Kidd—nineteen yesterday—and Bobby Charlton destroyed Benfica after they held United to 1—1 at ninety minutes.

European Cup Final	
MANCHESTER UNITED	4
BENFICA	1
After extra time	At Wembley

All the pre-match promises faded in the opening minutes when Benfica began to play with ruthless determination in defence.

The match had hardly begun when John Aston was pulled down by Graca on the edge of the penalty area only for Bobby Charlton's free kick to be cleared.

Full back Cruz was pinned tight to George Best and his first foul on the Irishman brought a word from Italian referee Lo Bello.

Almost immediately United had a chance when David Sadler went in behind the Benfica defence and side-footed at full stretch straight to goalkeeper Henrique.

Aston looked the best of United's forwards in the opening fifteen minutes and when he sprinted through on to a pass from Brian Kidd his centre just failed to find Pat Crerand.

The Portuguese tried to keep possession of the ball, stringing passes together while others sought space clear of United's defenders.

United did not pin one man to Eusebio but, like England in the World Cup, demanded that players pick him up in the middle of the field, while Stiles was detailed to mark him in and around United's penalty area.

The move worked well and it was twenty minutes before Eusebio had a chance.

Moved

United left him too much room close to goal and a tremendous right-foot shot came off the underside of Alex Stepney's crossbar before he had moved.

The fouls continued and referee Lo Bello did nothing to help the situation with some weird and unnecessary decisions.

They upset the players on both sides and the match developed an ugly pattern not in keeping with a great occasion.

Aston continued to be United's brightest forward, breaking past full back Adolfo as though he wasn't there.

When Benfica sensed that Lo Bello was ready to blow for anything skipper Coluna began to curl crosses to the edge of United's area.

It brought two free kicks for supposed fouls on the tall Torres that gave Eusebio a chance to threaten.

United now had their best chance as Sadler on a brilliant pass from Kidd went clean through only to pull his shot wide of Henrique's left hand post.

Then came a foul by Eusebio on Crerand which was bad enough to have had him sent off. The United half back was on the floor for four minutes receiving treatment.

United raised their game at the start of the second half, putting more pressure on the Portuguese in midfield.

Aston, who suffers derision at Old Trafford, almost made the match his own. His domination of Adolfo continually had Benfica in trouble.

It was from the left-hand side of the field that United struck, seven minutes into the second half.

Slanted

Full back Tony Dunne put Sadler clear with a short ball, and he manoeuvred into a space, to slant a centre into the penalty area.

Bobby Charlton rose to it, getting no more than a glance. But it was enough.

His header went in on the left-hand post with goalkeeper Henrique stranded in the middle of his goal.

Within minutes Best had the ball in the net again, only to be pulled back for an offside decision.

Eusebio came into the match as Benfica began to drive centres at the head of Torres.

It brought disaster for United in the seventy-eighth minute, as a cross from the right was headed downwards by Torres to Graca who put Benfica level.

As United's marking slackened off with their tiredness Eusebio began to get more opportunity and twice he might well have won the match in its dying minutes.

Fearsome

With three minutes left he was clean through hitting a fearsome shot that Stepney took low down to his right as the dusky Portuguese forward finished standing above him.

Just when it seemed as though United were ready to crack in extra time, they rose mightily to the occasion.

A long kick out of goalkeeper Stepney's hands was headed on by Kidd. Best squeezed the ball clear of a Portuguese defender and raced on.

As Henrique came off his line, Best swerved clear and gave United the goal that must have been like a massive injection of adrenalin.

Within two minutes Kidd, rising to a corner kick from the left, won and taken by Aston, gave United their third goal.

When Charlton sent Kidd clear along the right, he jumped clear of a vicious lunge by Cruz, and centred for Charlton to curl his shot across Henrique for United's fourth.

The crucial goals at Wembley

Graca, above, scores the equalising goal which took the final into extra time and right, Henriques, Benfica's goalkeeper, fails to reach Kidd's shot which brought United their third score

A great night for United

With the European Cup at last in their hands, Charlton (right) and Brennan lead Manchester United round Wembley

PELE SCORES 1,000TH GOAL IN TOP-CLASS FOOTBALL

1,000 UP!

Pele scores the goal the world has been waiting for

PELE, the boy who stole peanuts to pay for a football, has scored his 1,000th goal.

It was a penalty for Santos against Vasco da Gama before a 75,157 crowd at Rio's Maracana stadium. Hundreds invaded the pitch, and he was carried shoulder-high.

As Pele said, it was 'one of the greatest blessings a man could ever expect to receive from God.'

To all Brazil it was the final proof that one of its own sons had been the greatest player for a generation

Pele, born in the small town of Tres Coracoes 29 years ago, was as bad a schoolboy as Brazil has known. He spent more time kicking a football around the streets than he did in the classrooms before he was sent away to become a cobbler's apprentice.

But in 1958, after only two years in the game, he won the World Cup for Brazil in Sweden. British players were among those who stood back and wondered at the teen-ager's poise.

'It was his maturity and ball control you noticed,' said Jack Kelsey, goalkeeper of the Welsh side knocked out in the quarter-finals by Pele's goal.

'We'd never heard of him. It was all Didi and Vava then, but you could see he was a player. Mind you, his goal was a fluke.

Pele toured the world, scoring 80 goals each season while Santos collected £12,000 every time he played in front of crowds from Los Angeles to Leningrad.

Slowly, where fair means failed, defenders found other ways of stopping a player almost certain to score from every chance 20 yards out from goal.

He limped out of the 1966 World Cup at Liverpool, bruised and battered by European opponents determined to stifle his talent—and went home to worry.

'Nobody in the game had more fun than I did when I became a professional,' he said. 'This honeymoon had come to an abrupt end around 1960. I was continually marked the whole time I played and if I avoided the marking the boot went in.

He stuck to it, cushioned by a salary of £80,000 a year, matured by marriage, and kept in shape by not smoking or drinking.

After last night's celebrations he must look forward to the World Cup and a possible meeting with an England team who believe, like champions, that they can stop him.

'Of course he's a great player,' says centre-half Jackie Charlton. 'But he's playing in a part of the world where tackling is discouraged. We are certain we can deal with him.'

IAN ARCHER

AT LAST—PELE TAKES A 999 CALL TO GLORY

LATION as Pele walks off after making history.

IT WAS the first time, he said, he had ever trembled. He was called upon to take a penalty. More than 70,000 voices demanded that he take it. He held back.

"P-e-l-e . . . P-e-l-e . . ." they chanted. He still held back. Another voice over the public address system at the Maracana Stadium in Rio de Janeiro on Wednesday night insisted:

"Pele MUST kick. Pele MUST kick. Only after Pele scores his 1,000th goal will peace, calm and serenity return to Brazilian soccer fans."

Unpopular

They could have added: "to the whole of Brazil." He moved up to place the ball on the spot. The "peace" and "calm" arrived as the stadium hushed and stood like an empty shell.

By SUN REPORTER

He stepped back from the ball. It was hell for the guy. There had been 999 goals before, and few of them had bothered him.

But the country needed this goal—he needed it.

Andrada, the goalkeeper of Vasco da Gama, had his own thoughts. He had stopped earlier Pele efforts.

Now what was he to do? If he saved it he wouldn't be very popular. Nobody wanted him to save it, not even his own fans.

The world's most complete footballer moved forward and stroked the ball gently, ever so carefully, into the left-hand corner of the net.

He had scored it at last. The moment of "serenity" for a nation had come.

The crowd came on to the pitch and hoisted him onto their shoulders.

The 28-year-old genius, once a penniless boy in Tres Coracoes, Central Brazil, had passed a scoring milestone that no other footballer in the world had ever reached, or, I dare say, will ever reach.

He pulled a new jersey—numbered 1,000, naturally—over his playing shirt and embraced his team mates before going off so that the game could restart.

There were only 12 minutes play left. It was then that he said: "To-night was the first time I have ever trembled."

1,000 for Pele and the keeper knew the score

THE GOALKEEPER who failed to stop it was almost as proud as the man who scored it—for this was Pele's 1,000th goal in top-class football.

It came from a 78th-minute penalty as Santos played Vasco Da Gama in Rio De Janeiro's 150,000-seater Maracana Stadium. And Vasco 'keeper Norberto Andrada whipped off his jersey as the ball went in to reveal a silver shirt—with the figure 1,000 emblazoned across it.

ENGLAND LOSE TO BRAZIL IN MEMORABLE WORLD CUP CLASH IN 1970

OH, ENGLAND, ENGLAND!

England 0
Brazil 1

From BRIAN HITCHEN in Guadalajara

ENGLAND are right up against it. They lost their vital World Cup game against Brazil yesterday by the only goal of a wonderfully hard-fought match.

And Bobby Moore and his team—plus millions of fans viewing back home on TV—must be cursing the half-dozen chances missed by England's forwards in the match at Guadalajara.

Alan Ball and substitute Jeff Astle both shot wide, despite virtually open goals—as the fans' hearts pounded in excitement and disbelief.

But England are not beaten yet. Far from it.

Manager Sir Alf Ramsey was up and fighting almost before his team reached the changing rooms.

"I don't accept that we were the underdogs," he said. "Brazil were no better than we were.

"We lost because we did not take the opportunities that came our way."

Level

And Sir Alf was already planning a return game with the Brazilians—in the final.

But first England must play Czechoslovakia on Thursday in the game that could decide their World Cup future.

Rumania, who are level on points with England, have to play Brazil

But Sir Alf is confident England will win through to the quarter-finals. "I think the boys will soon recover from today's defeat," he added.

England captain Bobby Moore and Pele swap shirts after the match.

Jairzinho scores the only goal in the 60th minute for Brazil against England

ONE GOAL WRECKS UNLUCKY ENGLAND

GROUP THREE

BRAZIL .... **1 ENGLAND** **0**
Jairzinho HT: 0–0

(At Guadalajara)

	P	W	D	L	F	A	Pts
Brazil	2	2	0	0	5	1	4
England	2	1	0	1	1	1	2
Rumania	2	1	0	1	2	2	2
Czecho'vakia .	2	0	0	2	2	6	0

England missed Brazil didn't

(CHANCE AFTER CHANCE AFTER CHANCE)

England fail to snuff the spark of genius

From
ALBERT BARHAM
Guadalajara, June 7

Brazil, the old masters of slow, slow, quick, quick, slow, triumphed here today. Only one goal was scored, by the little butterfly winger Jairzinho after an hour. It was sufficient to remind England that they have never yet beaten Brazil in their own hemisphere. It was sad for England supporters, but it is not the end of the world. England can still qualify for the quarter-finals by beating Czechoslovakia on Thursday—even drawing if Rumania lose o Brazil on Wednesday.

Now Brazil almost certainly eem to be heading towards inning the group, and playing he quarter-finals here. Only ictory over them by the umanians and victory by Engnd over Czechoslovakia could ake this a three-way tie in hich goal difference would unt, and even then Brazil ve a fair advantage in goals.

England played their hearts t under the noon-day sun, and the thunder flashes burst gland walked off ruefully. o great chances were missed as many minutes only four nutes after the Brazilians had red. The first miss was by l, who mis-kicked a pass n Astle, in front of the goal. n it was the turn of Astle, self. He failed to take antage of a terrible defen- mix-up involving Everaldo shot wide of an open goal. y were, as far as England e concerned, the greatest most costly missed chances ne World Cup.

ere had been much specun about the fragility of the lian defence and on the rability of Felix in goal. e it to say that England were unable to take advantage of it even though they swarmed around the Brazilian goal more and more as the game went on, trying to pressurise them into error.

This was a battle between England's methodical, defensive network and the gifted self-expression of Pele, Tostao—until he was replaced—Jairzinho, and Paulo Cezar, who today took the place of Gerson, the master mind of Brazil's attack against Czechoslovakia, who was injured.

No one could fault Banks. He pushed away insidiously swerving shots, first, from Paulo Cezar and later from Roberto, the substitute for Tostao. One admired but did not envy the task of Cooper, to smother Jairzinho. He and Wright both performed well, with Cooper trying a few of his attacks down the wing when circumstances permitted. Mullery held Pele well, as he had done in Rio a year ago. But one cannot budget for genius. There was one occasion when Pele eluded the England defence and played the ball off defenders' legs as one does a billiard ball off a cushion. Mullery came to England's rescue then, sweeping the ball away from him.

Labone more than held the threat from Tostao, and once again England were thankful to Moore for his cool, commanding generalship. But the forwards could not get going often enough. England's passing was not as accurate as might have been expected on an occasion of such importance as this. But for all the Brazilians' worry about Piazza and Brito, the centre-backs, they thwarted Hurst, and Peters was seldom able to make his ghost-like runs on the blind side. Lee, who had tried to bustle through and on one occasion early on had a good chance half-smothered by Felix, and Bobby Charlton, who had worked himself almost to a standstill in the middle of the field, were replaced by Bell and Astle immediately after the Brazilians had scored.

It was then that the two England chances came and were lost for ever. England were efficient but they were against something intangible, a method, if method it be called, where unexpectedly graceful yet deceptive moves suddenly built into moments of great danger. Such was the goal built on the hour and other moves before it. Rivelino to Tostao, to Pele, and on to Jairzinho, and England were beaten. It was so simple.

For once Bobby Charlton heard whistles of derision directed at him as he fastened on to Peter's pass and strode through. The crowd greeted his high shot in the same manner.

For a while it looked as though England had at last found the cracks in this defence, but it was not to be. The warning came in the 52nd minute with a shot from Paulo Cezar which Banks dived to turn round for a corner. Then in another of their quick bursts Pele and Tostao weaved through. Yet again the defensive web closed round them. Then, on the hour, came the goal which beat England.

After their two disastrous misses, England pressed on. But they had to walk off the field as the vanquished. There was no disgrace in that. It remains now for a great effort against the Czechs next week to ensure that England qualify for the quarter-final even if they have to go to Leon to play it. I'm sure England now will be only too glad to do that.

Sir Alf Ramsey, England's team manager, said after: "The best team did not win. Brazil were a very good team in an even match. They took their one chance which is where we failed. My players have something to go for now. We still have another chance to qualify against Czechoslovakia."

Zagallo, Brazil's manager, said his team would play to win in Wednesday's game against Rumania. "No one shall say we do not try to win. If we lost it will not be our fault," he said.

ENGLAND.—Banks; Wright, Cooper; Moore, Labone, Mullery; Ball, R. Charlton, Peters, Hurst, Lee.

BRAZIL. — Felix; Alberto, Brito; Piazza, Everaldo, Cesar; Clodoaldo, Rivelino, Jair, Tostao, Pele.

Referee: A. Klein (Israel).

BILLY BREMNER & KEVIN KEEGAN BECOME FIRST PLAYERS TO BE SENT OFF AT WEMBLEY

Bremner and Keega

I didn't butt him, say

Off, said the ref ...so Bremner and Keegan go shirtless into disgrace

It's war after Giles hits out

Leeds 1, Liverpool 1 By BRIAN MADLEY

Liverpool won 6—5 on penalties

LLY BREMNER, sent off with Kevin Keegan for fighting in e 56th minute at Wembley, said last night: "The linesman id I butted Keegan. I didn't, but I'm not going to bother to peal."

Bremner (Leeds and Scotland captain) and Keegan (England and verpool), are the first British players to be sent off at Wembley, and r Keegan it's his second dismissal in four days.

FIRST FLARE-UP — Referee Bob Matthewson books Liverpool defender Tommy Smith.

ent off in punch-up shock

he Leeds captain

PICTURES BY BRENDAN MONKS

MADNESS

SPORTS MIRROR

GET OFF!

By KEN MONTGOMERY

THE moment history was made. And Kevin Keegan (left) and Billy Bremner can't believe they are the first Football League players to be sent off at Wembley. But there's no mistaking Bolton referee Bob Matthewson as he bawls: "Get off, lads" after the Liverpool and Leeds stars had finished their Charity Shield punch up. Leeds' giant Gordon McQueen can't believe it either.

It took fifty-one years and fifty-eight minutes for it to happen. And Keegan and Bremner had to follow in the ignominious footsteps of the Argentinian Rattin, who found himself in early hot bath water during England's 1966 World Cup match when he became the first man ever sent off in a soccer match at Wembley.

'Head butted'

Keegan, sent off in Germany during a Liverpool friendly in midweek, said angrily: "That's the second time within a week that I have been sent off for doing nothing. I don't know why I was sent off. I feel I am being victimised."

Bremner said: "I was upended in the penalty box at a free-kick.

The linesman claimed I had head-butted Keegan: I just don't do things like that."

Liverpool won the game on penalty kicks after the Cup Winners and the Champions finished level at 1—1.

An ambulance man said, sardonically: "If that was the Charity Shield, God knows what the Cup Final's going to be like."

THE MEN WHO SHAMED WEMBLEY

SHAME ON THEM ALL

LEEDS captain Billy Bremner, shirtless, his head hung low, walks off the Wembley pitch yesterday after an astonishing punch-up with Kevin Keegan of Liverpool.

The referee and a linesman had to separate the pair during the F.A. Charity Shield match.

After the incident both players threw off their shirts in disgust.

Players and fans shock Soccer

It was a nasty moment in a match which had become a massive hooligan-busting operation for the police.

And it was hard to believe that this was a pre-season warm-up to the real thing—the League championship which starts next week.

Before the match chanting rowdies smashed up two bars in The Torch pub near the stadium, forcing the landlord to close an hour and a half early at 1 p.m.

Invasion

Landlord, Mr Clive Lambourne, 38, said afterwards: "It was terrifying. We are close to the ground, and we normally expect some trouble, but this is the worst we have ever had.

"There were two or three thousand of them in the pub, the gardens, and the road outside.

"It was like an invasion. They smashed hundreds of glasses, ripped the wall fittings off, and smashed furniture."

Damage costing about £1,000 was caused.

Meanwhile a special troubleshooter cops squad arrested 13 fans at the turnstiles.

And the 60,000 fans who got into the ground faced random checks and searches for offensive weapons.

Football fans arriving at Hull for the friendly match between Manchester United and Hull City also found police out in force.

Many had travelled from Manchester on a "dry" train on which drinks were banned.

Eleven young fans were arrested following incidents during and after yesterday's friendly match between Reading and Oxford, at Elm Park, Reading.

Those arrested will appear in court this week.

Wembley match report—Page 20.

SOCCER OFF DAY

LIVERPOOL COMPLETE A LEAGUE AND UEFA CUP DOUBLE IN MAY 1976

SALUTE THE CHAMPS

REDS

Champagne time for triumphant Liverpool aft r their record ninth championship success.

RANGERS PIPPED!

REDS RULE, OK!
FRANK McGHEE
PAGES 26, 27

RULE, O.K.!

Liverpool do it in style

FRANK McGHEE
THE VOICE OF SPORT

Wolves 1, Liverpool 3

LIVERPOOL won theilr ninth First Division championship—a record —the way all important titles should be decided: with skill and spirit and power and confidence.

The happy hordes of shouting, singing "Reds" fans who stormed the Molineux picth at the final whistle last night were, in that marvellous demonstration of affection, saluting all those special qualities.

Anfield transported its famous Kop en masse to the Midlands, taking over the Wolverhampton ground as completely as, in the end, their team took over the match.

That, it must be emphasised, was never easy. Wolves, who lost their own First Division place last night, made it an uphill fight for most of the way after a shock early goal from Steve Kindon in the thirteenth minute

What really made it so memorable from then on was Liverpool's determination not to allow that shock to disturb their massive composure, ruin their rhythm or affect their attitude of complete certainty.

There were only fourteen minutes left when Kevin Keegan equalised, but there had not been even a trace of anxiety until then.

Clinched

And although a draw would have been enough to take the title on goal average, Liverpool would not settle for that. They wanted the clear-cut victory that further goals from John Toshack and Ray Kennedy clinched in the closing stages of a story that deserves and demands to be told as it happened.

Wolves made it clear from the start that they weren't readily accepting the role of victims. Their own unexpected early pressure, in fact, forced the error that could haunt Liverpool centre half Phil Thompson for years.

As he missed an easy interception, Wolves striker Kindon flashed past him—and this man can move. No one got within tackling distance as he raced on to strike the ball sweetly and powerfully into the net.

Many, probably most First Division teams might have crumpled in the pressure-cooker tension of that situation—and it became worse as the misses mounted.

Kennedy, the big midfield man who spread his own composure like a cloak around the rest of his colleagues, was unlucky three times-

Even the arrival of the red-haired David Fairclough as substitute for Jimmy Case in the 65th minute failed to have its usual galvanising effect.

Nothing was going right until the dramatic 76th minute equaliser. Tommy Smith, crowning a great season at full-back when so many had written him off, lifted a long ball diagonally into the penalty area for the tall Toshack to flick on with a typical back-header which placed Keegan so completely in the clear he was able to run the ball into the net.

Suspicion

There was, I felt, a suspicion of offside about the second goal in the 85th minute. A linesman quite clearly had his flag up throughout the move.

But Toshack did perform brilliantly to leave behind Wolves full-back Geoff Palmer with an intricate swivel before scoring.

There were no arguments, however, about the merit of the result or the quality of the final goal — a marvellous Keegan dribble followed by a pass to Kennedy, who shot hard and high into the roof of the net.

LIVERPOOL CLINCH IT!

Bruges 1, Liverpool 1 (Aggregate: 3-4)

EMLYN HUGHES, the Liverpool skipper, was so jubilant, so triumphant when he received the UEFA Cup to add to the League Championship trophy last night that he promptly dropped it!

DEREK WALLIS at the UEFA Cup Final

It was one of the few mistakes his side made in a thoroughly professional performance that suggests the European Cup itself may not be beyond them next season.

There are not many teams in Europe better equipped than Bruges yet Liverpool, facing a delicate situation with a fragile 3—2 lead from the first leg, dealt with them unhurriedly, unworriedly as for the second time in three years they completed the League and UEFA Cup double.

Carnival

Once the tension of the 90 minutes had lifted, it became a night of carnival for Liverpool who swapped shirts with their opponents, danced rather than ran on the lap of honour, and paid a special, moving tribute to their colony of supporters at one end of the ground.

Seldom has a team been more deserving of the honours that have poured on them this season.

Champion of champions, with a record ninth title win, Manager of the Year in Bob Paisley, Player of the Year in Kevin Keegan and five men in the England squad . . . that is the impressive list of qualifications that Liverpool will take with them into the European Cup

All right, so this particular performance was composed rather than colourful, sound instead of spectacular, but some teams might have foundered when in the disastrous 11th minute Tommy Smith conceded a penalty by handling the ball and Lambert scored from the spot.

That goal could have been the killer coming as it did so early in the game, and levelling the score on aggregate. Yet Liverpool were far from downhearted. Within five minutes they retrieved an awkward situation by regaining their one-goal lead.

Fooled

From a free-kick awarded outside the penalty area, Hughes fooled the defensive wall by playing the ball short and square to Keegan, who drilled a right-foot shot unerringly to equalise.

Liverpool could hardly have had greater encouragement, because this was the first goal Bruges had conceded at home in the UEFA Cup this season.

Liverpool had to keep a close watch on the lively Lambert and Van Gool, but as confidence mounted they played the ball unhurriedly out of defence and constructed attacks expertly as if reminding Bruges that that they were not there simply to soak up punishment.

Tommy Smith almost put Liverpool ahead after 34 minutes, when, with the referee ignoring a linesman's flag, he advanced to meet Ray Kennedy's free-kick with a volley that flew agonisingly wide.

Liverpool almost cracked five minutes into the second half, when a move involving Le Fevre and Van Gool split the defence, leaving Lambert with a vicious shot that beat Clemence but bounced off his left-hand post.

Liverpool lived dangerously but somebody was always there to deal with awkward situations — usually Thompson.

And when the defence was breached four minutes from time, Ray Clemence retrieved his reputation after the error that cost England the match against Scotland with a superb diving save from Cools.

RESULTS

UEFA CUP FINAL
(second leg)

BRUGES ....1 **LIVERPOOL** ...1
Lambert (pen) Keegan
H-T: 1—1 30,000
Agg.: Liverpool win 4—3

WELSH CUP FINAL
(second leg)

CARDIFF .....3 **HEREFORD** ...2
Pethard, Clark, T. Evans Lindsay, Byrne
H-T: 2—0 2,648
Agg.: Cardiff win 6—5.

Keegan climbs every mountain to put Liverpool on summit

UEFA Cup final—second leg

After Bayern . . . it's Liverpool

From PAUL WILCOX: Bruges 1, Liverpool 1 (agg 3-4)

Bruges, May 19

Liverpool repeated their feat of 1973 when they added the UEFA cup to their League title after walking a defensive tightrope in the second leg of the final against the Belgian champions.

For organisation and method, Liverpool could hardly be faulted — especially when it is considered that they lost their balance and their aggregate lead as early as the 11th minute.

And while a great deal of their possession play brought jeers and cat calls from the Belgian supporters as Bruges attempts to attack were stifled, Liverpool at least had provided fair warning that they were not out to win any friends. Just the cup—and they did that.

If Bayern Munich can take the Champions Cup from the back, why should Liverpool be castigated? They did all that they said they would, and had the verve and skill to shrug off the early goal to become the first team to score against the Belgians at home in the competition this season.

Liverpool's plans were disrupted when Smith handled to give away a penalty but they took less than four minutes to equalise, fittingly through the superb Keegan and then Thompson and Hughes repulsed almost everything the Belgians could throw. With forwards helping out in defence, it might not have been pretty, but for effectiveness Liverpool would have been a match for anyone.

Liverpool revised their policy when Bruges were awarded their penalty. Lambert and Cools, the scorers of Bruges two goals at Anfield in the first leg, exposed the rigid marking system for the first and last time with delightful interchange of passes around the edge of the penalty area. But with Cools shaping to shoot, Smith stuck out an arm as the ball bounced for a possible volley, and Lambert's shot was high into the net.

Considering the away goals rule, Liverpool had no option but to attack, with Keegan guiding their forward moves, but they could hardly have expected to equalise so quickly. After 15 minutes Krieger was penalised on the edge of the area for dangerous kicking, and Hughes's short square pass to his right was rifled home by Keegan. That was all that was needed to restore Liverpool's balance, and they fell back into the containing role for which they had planned. Hughes and Thompson were fully occupied, and four minutes after the interval the Belgians' undoubted talents were shown without any tangible reward. With Liverpool pressed back, Van Cool carved a path for Lambert with a majestic through ball and the Belgian striker shrugged off Thompson's challenge for putting a shot that cannoned off the near post with Clemence beaten.

There were further scares for Liverpool but Thompson and Hughes were towers of strength under pressure. After 62 minutes Fairclough replaced Toshack as Liverpool's often lone raider. Bruges made two substitutions taking off De Cubba for Henderyck after 68 minutes and replacing the limping Lambert with Sanders seven minutes later but it availed them little as Liverpool, drawing on their experience of 12 successive seasons of European competition kept finding ways to thwart the Belgians attacks.

BRUGES: Jensen; Bastijns, Krieger, Leekens, Volders, Cools, Vandereycken, Van Gool, Lambert, De Cubber, Le Fevre.

LIVERPOOL: Clemence; Smith, Neal, Thompson, Kennedy, Hughes, Keegan, Case Heighway, Toshak, Callaghan.

Referee: Rudi Glockner (E Germany).

Keegan (left), of England, and Toshack, of Wales, successful to the end as a combination for Liverpool.

ENGLAND'S 1986 WORLD CUP DREAMS SHATTERED BY ARGENTINA IN HISTORIC MATCH

It's 'adios' to Mexico

Lineker again . . . Gary turns away after netting his consolation goal

The tough get tougher . . . England defender Kenny Sansom tussles with Jorge Valdano

ENGLAND'S DESTROYER: Diego Maradona, who scored both Argentina's goals

Maradona puts out England

TWO second-half goals by Argentina's Diego Maradona put England out of the Mexico World Cup last night. Gary Lineker scored his sixth goal of the competition with a header nine minutes before the end to make it 2-1.

Controversy surrounded Maradona's first goal, in the 51st minute, with claims that he had put the ball in the net with his hand. However, four minutes later he collected the ball just inside England's half and beat several defenders before shooting past Peter Shilton.

Lineker's goal came after a cross by John Barnes. England's best chance of an equaliser came from the same combination but Lineker just failed to reach another cross from the left.

Report, page 28.

Sleight of hand: the controversial moment when Maradona gave Argentina a helping hand in their victory over England

Maradona finds

Diego Maradona ended England's World Cup run here in Mexico City yesterday when he broke the resistance of Bobby Robson's defenders with two goals in five minutes early in the second half to set his team on the way to the semi-finals for the second time in three tournaments.

England went out bravely and even looked like saving the game after Lineker had met a cross from Barnes nine minutes from the end to score his sixth goal of the competition. With three minutes to go he was only inches away from repeating the feat although in between times Tapia had hit a post for Argentina. In the end few could deny that the winners had given a thoroughly professional performance.

Dealing with Maradona was always going to be a problem. Tackling him within scoring range was akin to challenging someone carrying a live hand grenade — hit or miss, the result was always likely to be explosive.

Not that Argentina came equipped to mount an immediate offensive, starting the game with Paculli, a striker, on the bench, and Enrique recalled to stiffen the midfield. With Fenwick back after suspension and Reid fit, England began with the side that had beaten Poland 3-0 in Monterrey.

Before the kick-off each England player received a pennant from a member of the Argentine team. Unless they bore the words Malvinas Argentinas it was a nice gesture and Fenwick's first tackle on Maradona after 10 minutes was less diplomatic. After the Argentinian had gone flying the England defender was cautioned for the third time in the tournament.

It seemed a little harsh, being England's first foul of the game, but then Maradona is Maradona. At least his free kick was nothing special, Shilton clearing the ball from under the bar after it had taken a deflection off the wall.

At the other end there was more anxiety when Pumpido slipped as he went out wide to his left to meet Beardsley. Fortunately for the Argentinians the England striker was too badly placed to manage anything more than a speculative shot into the side netting.

With the midfield crowded and the teams setting out to close each other down, the game was not unlike an average First Division fixture. Fenwick's tackle notwithstanding, England did not appear to be setting out to mark Maradona individually. Instead, they concentrated on interrupting his lines of communications with his team mates.

Space was hard to find in either half and the crowd, becoming bored with the spectacle, began to make their own amusement, rising in turn to send the now familiar wave of movement round the stadium like wind blowing across a cornfield.

Two more free kicks from Maradona drew their attention back to the arena but little came of them. Nevertheless Maradona was becoming more of an influence and while England had not conceded any goal by half-time it was obvious they still had a lot of defending to do. Moreover, the chance of finding Lineker or Beardsley in meaningful position near goal was becoming slimmer by the minute.

The second half began with an isolated outburst of fighting at one end of the stadium where English and Argentinian supporters had been singing in more or less peaceful co-existence. This was still being sorted out by the police when Maradona virtually won the match for Argentina with two goals in the 50th and 54th minutes.

First he ploughed into the heart of the England defence before laying the ball off to his right. It came off Hodge and looped into the air. Maradona reacted first and as he went up for it with Shilton he appeared to knock it over the goalkeeper with a hand.

However if there was any doubt about that goal there was absolutely none about the next. After collecting the ball wide on the right Maradona went through the English defence with such speed and skill that he left a trail of fallen players behind him. Stevens was beaten by a subtle swerve, Butcher by a sway of the hips and Fenwick with contemptuous ease before Maradona finally slipped the ball passed Shilton. Bobby Robson had said beforehand that Maradona was capable of winning a game on his own in five minutes and now, to England's cost, the little man had taken him at his word.

All Enland could do now was throw everything into attack and with Waddle and Barnes replacing Reid and Steven this is what they did. Argentina's defence looked shaky as Pumpido had to move quickly to turn a free kick from Hoddle round a post. Maradona meanwhile had collected a reproof from Fenwick who, if he had been unfortunate to be cautioned earlier, was now lucky to stay on the field.

England: **Shilton** (Southampton), **Stevens** (Everton), **Sansom** (Arsenal), **Fenwick** (Queen's Park Rangers), **Butcher** (Ipswich Town), **Steven** (Everton), **Hoddle** (Tottenham Hotspur), **Reid** (Everton), **Hodge** (Aston Villa), **Beardsley** (Newcastle United), **Lineker** (Everton).

Substitutes: **Woods** (Norwich City), **Stevens** (Tottenham Hotspur), **Wilkins** (AC Milan), **Barnes** (Watford), **Waddle** (Tottenham Hotspur).

ARGENTINA: Pumpido; Cuciuffo, Brown, Ruggeri, Olarticoechea, Giusti, Batista, Burruchaga, Enrique, Maradona, Valdano.

Substitutes: Islas, Clausen, Pasculli, Tapia, Trobbiani.

Referee: Ali Ben Naceur (Tunisia).

FALL

e knockout punch

PRIDE . . . Fenwick downs the man who did the same to England — Maradona

THE MARADONA ROW GOES

'We went out to a cheat'

ENGLAND skipper Bryan Robson headed ou of Mexico yesterday insisting: "We were cheated."

The Diego Maradona handball incident whic brought about England's World Cup exit was still th big talking point as the players packed their bags.

Argentina's 2-1 win to reach tomorrow's semi-finals was painful enough, but the debate grew into whether Maradona is generally a cheat and con man.

True, he's marked by hatchet men, often brutally hacked to pieces. But on many occasions he dives to fool the referee into awarding free kicks in dangerous positions.

Sidelined skipper Robson, watching England fall to Maradona's handled first goal, felt Tunisian referee Ali Bennaceur should shoulder the responsibility.

Pace

Maradona's cheating was bad enough, but the real crime was the ref's failure to stop it.

Robson said: "It was handball and everyone bar the referee must have seen it. I don't see how a referee from Tunisia, with not much experience, could be in control of a World Cup quarter-final. He should have seen it.

"The lads have done well. Young ones have come in, gained valuable experience, and I don't think we've let anyone down. My big regret is simply the way we wer out."

Even Maradona conce ed yesterday: "The fir goal was the work of th hand of God."

Team-mate Jorge Va dano said: "Diego felt s bad about the first go that he had to come u with the brilliant second

The darker side of Ma adona's game had si goal England striker Ga Lineker saying: "He's great player who has e erything. He doesn't ne to resort to that kind behaviour."

Defender Terry F wick, who was booked

KILLER BLOW: Maradona clearly handles.

ON AS ENGLAND FLY HOME

THE CON MAN

WORLD CUP INQUEST

the opening minutes for fouling Maradona, stormed: "He cons referees. I don't just mean the goal he knocked in with his hand.

"Go near him and down he goes. He's got fantastic pace and skill, but spoils it by cheating.

"With his ability he doesn't need to do it. Pele and Cryuff were great players, but you never saw them do the sort of things Maradona does.

Peter Shilton, directly involved in the 50th-minute goal, was almost inconsolable.

He said: "Maradona was never going to get the ball, so he took a chance and punched it in.

"You have to rely on the referee and linesman to see it. They were not doing their job properly.

"They were running back together looking at each other, neither knowing what to do"

WHAT A WAY TO GO!

'Handball' goal storm